PARENTING FROM THE PASSENGER SEAT

Enjoy the ride!

Pam Roy

PARENTING FROM THE PASSENGER SEAT

How Our Children Develop Capabilities, Connections, and Meaningful Lives

PAM ROY

Co-Founder, B-Unbound

VFIA
VIKTOR FRANKL INSTITUTE
OF AMERICA PUBLISHING

VIKTOR FRANKL INSTITUTE OF AMERICA PUBLISHING
LOS ANGELES, CALIFORNIA, USA

VFIA Publishing
Los Angeles, California

Cataloging-in-Publication Data is on file with the Library of Congress
Paperback ISBN: 978-1-7348862-2-1
eBook ISBN: 978-1-7348862-3-8
Audiobook: 978-1-7348862-4-5

Book cover design by Ian Robinson
Book cover illustration by Blue Seat Studios
Interior design by Christina Thiele
Editorial production by KN Literary Arts

PassengerSeatParent.com

To my daughters, Emily, Rachel, and Allison,
who inspired me to become myself

CONTENTS

INTRODUCTION: AWAKENING TO A NEW PERSPECTIVE

If you picked up this book, you probably already sense that something is wrong with how we raise and educate our children. You are not alone—I sensed it too. Like me, you may be a parent overwhelmed by the educational demands placed on your children and questioning whether the standardized approach prepares them for life in a rapidly changing world. These issues, and my concern about the mental health crisis affecting so many young people, motivated me to write this book. I want to share my search to understand what is happening to our children in the name of education and the discoveries I made along the way. I also want to recommend potential solutions to fix the quandary we find ourselves in, along with ways we can work together to promote health and well-being for all children.

I came to parenting late in life. I married at age 35 and was 41 when the youngest of my three daughters was born. The forty-year gap between my childhood experiences and my children's, especially the role school played in our lives, highlighted an alarming shift for me. School was part of my growing-up years, but it was not central to my life the way it is for today's kids. The mass production model of schooling was prevalent back then, but there was still a broad array of socially acceptable options after high school. We worked part-time jobs or otherwise engaged with our community during the year. The college-for-all mantra had not yet gained steam, and most of us did not compete with our peers for grades, test scores, awards, or admissions. I am not suggesting that my schooling years were a beneficial time for all—they weren't. But neither do I believe that the shift to forcing everyone through the same narrow college door has benefited most children, and we can all see that it has not created a healthy society.

My parents were first-generation Americans. My immigrant grandparents came to the U.S. from Italy and Sweden, searching for a better life after World War I. They were laborers working in orchards, factories, and construction. My father went to a state college, and my mother was a homemaker. After serving in the Navy, my father climbed the corporate ladder as an engineer-turned-manager, and our family's socio-economic status improved considerably during my upbringing. I was one of three daughters; two of us attended college, and one did not.

My own post–high school path was meandering. I dropped out of junior college twice while working minimum-wage jobs. I went to a state college for a year before transferring and graduating from the University of Southern California with a degree in Business in 1981. (I would not qualify for admission today.) I paid for college with student loans and help from my parents. I entered the field of real estate market research and consulting. It was a time when, if you had a degree, you generally got a well-paying job—unlike today. Growing up during the 1970s feminist movement, I felt a strong push to invest in my career and embraced it wholeheartedly.

I checked all the boxes for society's vision of success by the time I was 30—degree, management position, car, condo—but I still felt an emptiness. I thought to myself, *This is it? The promised payoff?* Soon after hitting a physical and emotional wall, I changed my life dramatically to realign with my authentic values. I married and finally lived my dream of having children. Emily was born in 1997, Rachel in 1999, and Allison in 2001. In many ways, I feel like the life I was meant to lead began when I became a mother. My experience following societal definitions of success and the resulting void shaped how I viewed my children's childhoods and the focus on academic achievement.

2

In addition, I was fortunate to marry an entrepreneur who had started a business in his garage that rose to international success. I was provided with choices and opportunities not afforded to most parents.

Given my years of experience in the workplace, this financial freedom also allowed me to step back and closely evaluate whether the promised academic trajectory would deliver a fulfilling life for my children. Most importantly, I questioned the cost of time lost in the present moment; the emotional toll of being confined to buildings in mind, body, and spirit for hours on end; and the disconnection from mentor relationships, community engagement, and exploration. I couldn't understand why children were required to devote so much of their young lives to learning a theoretical version of real life while the world was rapidly transforming all around them.

THE TENTACLES OF SCHOOL

As my children entered their schooling years at a parochial school, our lives took on a frantic rhythm of activities and homework. The lines between home and school became blurred, and I was expected to enforce all school mandates. I felt increasingly uncomfortable and frustrated that the tentacles of school could encroach into our home life and demand my children's free time. It seemed ridiculous to me that filling in blank spaces on a worksheet or memorizing formulas for a test could be considered more valuable than time spent exploring their interests, learning through a variety of experiences, and nurturing their relationships, especially with aging grandparents. I realized that these mandates were not unique to any type of public or private school; they had become the social norm.

In 2005, when my first two daughters were still in the early part of elementary school and my youngest in preschool, I met with the school principal and expressed my concerns about the stated homework expectations and the limitations that placed on their childhoods.

Not all parents are comfortable speaking up, but I think it is important that we respectfully push back against school demands on our children's time if we believe it is unhealthy. I shared my view that children were demanded to allocate more than the forty-hour work week required of adults. Homework was regularly added to the seven-hour school day (eight hours with going to and from school), and sports or after-school activities consumed even more time. I stated my belief that this approach to treating children like programmable robots and mini-adults was detrimental to their health and well-being.

In a follow-up email, I noted:

> *If we start them this young, then push them for extra time in high school, then college, then they work, then they have families, what have we taught them about the value of relationships? This hamster wheel approach never ends. What are we modeling about life? Are they better, happier, and more motivated to serve their families and communities because of what they know and their academic achievements?*

If we look around, we can see the resulting burnout, disengagement, and exhaustion by the time children reach high school.

The principal acknowledged my points and expressed concern. But, in the end, she felt compelled to meet the state-mandated academic outcomes necessary to maintain the school's "Blue Ribbon" status. By the time my youngest daughter began kindergarten, I could no longer ignore the warning bells in my head, telling me that this was not a healthy lifestyle for my children. I knew we had to make a change. It was not a decision we made lightly. We were leaving a tribe and venturing into the world on our own, against the cultural tide, but the discomfort of leaving the familiar surroundings had to be pushed aside if we were to honor our values.

I evaluated the limited choices available at the time, such as homeschooling and a couple of small independent schools, but they didn't feel like the right options. (Today, dozens of types of schooling options are available in my area as well as more socially active homeschooling groups.) Ideally, I wanted the flexibility and shorter instruction time homeschooling offered but in a brick-and-mortar setting with a variety of classes to choose from, teachers teaching subjects they loved to teach, and multi-age student engagement. I was fortunate to have the resources to explore alternatives that best fit my children as many parents don't.

A few months later, I stood in the school parking lot talking with some moms and learned of a new, for-profit school where a mutual friend had moved her children. I immediately called, found out the name, and visited. The small K–8 school was located in an office building with a public park down the street. It offered three multi-age classrooms, long breaks for recess and lunch, no standardized testing or multiple-choice questions, a six-hour day, and a stated "no home-work" policy. While students had to read each night and prepare for tests, there was none of the endless busywork. My daughters switched schools the next month.

Friends and family were very concerned that my children would not be adequately prepared for college since they weren't doing the things supposedly required for admission. Despite pressures to follow the cultural norms, we did our best to stay true to our values and priorities. As it turned out, none of the academic or sports achievements that were supposedly missing from their elementary and middle school résumés affected any of my daughters' acceptances to "good colleges." They even managed to find their way into specialty programs in their colleges and graduate in four years, and one completed a Master's Degree. The myth did not live up to the reality.

When it came time for high school, we told our children that they could attend one of three high schools within a fifteen-minute radius of our home. I didn't think any of their public or private options were better than another as they all followed the state-mandated curricula, and college résumé mania was inescapable in our community. I wanted them to invest themselves where they felt most comfortable.

My eldest daughter chose an independent private school, and her sisters soon followed. There, I noticed the significant emotional and physical distress of students who were all required to follow the same narrow track while constantly competing with each other. The students all needed to comply and conform to administrator, teacher, and coach dictates, both at school and at home.

As most of the families had resources, the emphasis of the students' daily lives during the school year and in the summer was on preparing for college admissions. Although the school was relatively small and had dedicated college counselors, many parents hired private services to help with college applications and essays. I wanted my daughters to prepare their own applications so that they would reflect who they were, not some idealized candidate. It was a chaotic time for our family. I was exhausted trying to balance what I felt was necessary for my children's well-being and their strong desire to follow along with what their friends were doing.

During this time, I was actively volunteering with foster youth programs and served on the board of a nonprofit foundation. I saw firsthand the emotional distress of these foster youth as they were moved from school to school and the difficulty they had in keeping up with academic demands. Getting to know these youth and those in my more affluent, achievement-oriented community showed me that being constrained and controlled by others—no matter how well-meaning—resulted in similar experiences with anxiety, depression, aggression, addiction, and despair.

I noticed that the rigid structures placed around their lives afforded neither of these youth groups the time nor the freedom to engage with their communities or pursue things they were interested in. It turns out that both too little and too much attention leaves students unseen and unheard as unique and valuable individuals. I began to realize that this was a societal issue created by the very framework of our education system.

While raising my children, I read *Man's Search for Meaning* by renowned psychiatrist Viktor Frankl. His meaning-oriented philosophy resonated strongly with my value system and has influenced my life choices and decisions. As I learned more about the critical role meaning plays in our lives and how it is *specific* to the individual, I realized that this is the exact opposite of how we educate children in our standardized system. No wonder there is so much palatable distress! I was particularly interested in Frankl's finding that meaning is a key factor in mental health and well-being. Little did I know that my advocacy efforts would soon lead me to dive deep into his work and help start The Viktor E. Frankl Institute of America with his grandson.

QUESTIONING COLLEGE-FOR-ALL

While I continually had an uneasy feeling about the negative impact the long road to college admissions was having on children, I didn't really question the path we were all on until I went back to college myself. My concern about the rise in youth anxiety, depression, cutting, eating disorders, addiction, and suicide that I was seeing in my community, reading about in books and articles, and hearing about from friends across the country, led me to pursue an online Master's Degree in School Counseling.

I hadn't thought about getting a Master's Degree, but the opportunity presented itself when my youngest daughter, Allison, was a freshman in high school and expressed interest in a summer program at an elite East Coast university. As I was looking at the broad range of programs targeted to high school students on their website, an advertisement promoting a brand-new online Master's Degree popped out at me. I applied. It turned out that the real reason Allison was trying to get to New York was that she wanted to see Justin Bieber at Madison Square Garden. She did not end up attending the school, but I did.

My goal was not to become a school counselor, but I thought

the required yearlong internship in a school setting would provide me with an invaluable perspective. I hoped to become a stakeholder liaison advocating on behalf of students with parents, administrators, teachers, and the community. And so, at 56 years old, I embarked on a journey into the world of higher education that would change the trajectory of my life.

With one daughter in college, two in high school preparing for college, and me in graduate school, I was immersed in every level of the college process. And at that point, I still thought college was the correct pathway for my children. We had started college savings accounts for each of them right when they were born and followed the cultural mandate that college was necessary for any advancement in life.

Some of my classes were thought-provoking, but others were heavy in content made irrelevant by the internet and dramatic economic change. I thought I would be learning from tenured professors, but instead, we mostly viewed them on videos and were taught by adjunct professors.

During the two-year program, we were required to attend a four-day immersion where I had the opportunity to meet my classmates in person after months of seeing each other online. I was significantly older than most of them and enjoyed the intergenerational engagement. As I got to know my classmates, I became aware of the financial struggles many were experiencing. Most weren't staying in the hotel offered for the immersion because it was too expensive—they stayed at youth hostels, couch surfed, or commuted in from neighboring areas. Our dinner conversations highlighted some of their journeys as the first in their families to attend college and the heavy burden of student loans.

With a background in finance, I tried to understand the cost/benefit of attending the program. When I entered in 2016, the cost of the Master's Degree was $81,000. The median school counseling job paid $57,000.[1] With a full-time commitment to school for the two years required, the "opportunity cost" of not earning an income was high. Many of my classmates lost the potential income of a college graduate ($50,000 per year times two years),[2] bringing the real cost to $181,000. How could this make sense, especially since many of them (and most graduate students) also carried undergraduate debt?

The next thing that surprised me was how disconnected the curriculum was from the changing educational environment. The material taught ignored that schools today vary widely in how they address student needs and allocate their budgets. Academic advisors (requiring an Associate's Degree) rather than school counselors (requiring a Master's Degree) are being hired at many schools. Also, because of school shootings in recent years, some schools allocate their budget to security guards rather than counselors.

We were taught a very rigid structure for the school counselor role that included three components: academic advising, career guidance, and social-emotional support. In reality, the ratio of students to school counselors is exceptionally high across the country—from 186:1 in Vermont to 716:1 in Arizona[3]—leaving little time for the necessary attention to students for each of these components.

The need for crisis intervention in schools is essential, but I began thinking that the system's structured approach to unique human beings was a significant contributor to student distress. As Gandhi observed, children need vocational experiences for well-rounded development because it relieves them *"from the tyranny of purely academic and theoretical instruction against which their active nature is always making a healthy protest."* Addressing the framework of the system itself is critical for prevention and desperately needed.

After finishing the required coursework (30 units), I was ready for my pre-internship practicum. The closest school they could find for me was a two- to three-hour drive in heavy traffic. As I still had two children at home, I declined to do this twice a week and took it upon myself to find something else in my community.

I found an opportunity at a nonprofit counseling center embedded in a local public high school of 3,000 students. The school had one full-time and one part-time counselor with seven academic advisors. The center—created by a coalition of community-based mental health specialists, law enforcement, the high school principal, and other concerned citizens—actively provided socio-emotional support to students. Although it worked in conjunction with the school counselors, it was run by licensed social workers, and I had to be granted special permission from my program directors to join them. I learned a lot from the amazing, dedicated executive director, Susan Parmelee, and the students I had the opportunity to meet.

When it came time for me to serve my yearlong internship, however, my program would not allow me to continue to work at the nonprofit center run by social workers, as they did not follow the strict degree guidelines set forth by an independent accreditation agency. The fact that these centers are growing in response to the demand for counseling services and working closely with the school counselors made me realize how accreditation was a significant factor limiting the ability of colleges to respond to the transforming economy. It also made me rethink the value of sending every student through the current bureaucratic college system when every aspect of the way we live and work is dramatically changing.

It was during a meeting I attended with a school counselor, school district psychologist, and the parents of a depressed sophomore student that I realized I couldn't spend a year of my life in the school system. The parents described their son's boredom with the eighty-minute block classes and his unwillingness to get out of bed. They said he complained that the material didn't relate to his life. The counseling protocol was to help get him "back on track" by providing extra tutoring and alternative classes for support. The view was that his depression would be helped through adjustments to his academic program.

By this time, with all I had come to learn about the vast disconnect between school and the real world and the critical role meaning plays in mental health, I thought to myself, *This student is perfect; the system is flawed! He is having a normal reaction to the devaluing of his uniqueness and is rebelling against our culture of sameness.*

I am not against college for those who have mature life skills and require it for their chosen path, but its current structure of mass-processing students for predetermined degrees does not serve the vast majority of people. It is too costly and limits both exploration and potential. Checking boxes someone else sets does little to prepare our children to follow their own intuitive decision-making abilities as they learn to navigate their way throughout life.

DECIDING TO CONTRIBUTE

My efforts to contribute to positive change have led me into areas I never expected. When my frustration with the dehumanizing schooling approach peaked and I decided not to complete my internship, my friend and fellow mom, Cara Cragun, suggested that I start a parenting blog. She said she was interested in learning how to build a website (using YouTube videos) and volunteered to edit my blog posts. She also agreed to handle my social media posts, which were necessary to reach an audience. (I had been rebelling against social media because I felt it was negatively impacting my children, so I had no familiarity with how to use it.)

I had only written reports and letters but agreed to try. I felt so vulnerable putting my ideas and thoughts into a public forum for scrutiny. But my concern about what was happening to children in the name of education made me override my fears. I felt strongly that I needed to challenge the ongoing narrative. Without Cara, I never would have started my blog—creatively titled Pam Roy Blog because I couldn't think of anything else at that moment—and the incredible partnerships and adventures it has brought into my life.

Yes, I became a grad school dropout. I started writing blogs for parents, sharing my newfound perspective and research, discussing the maturity and focus needed for college, expressing concern about the confinement of children, and raising awareness of the escalating mental health crisis our society helped create. I also highlighted the many alternative pathways that were rapidly emerging, pathways that allowed students to explore possibilities *before* investing time and money into a college degree—if one was even needed for their desired pursuit.

Another close friend, Moira Hummel, a lawyer, parent, grandparent, critical thinker, and avid reader, offered to be my content editor. She reviewed each blog post before it was published, and we had many lively debates that helped me hone my craft. Within a few months, I received positive feedback from my blog readers and was asked to contribute to some publications. The writing of the blog ushered in unexpected new chapters in my life, as I describe throughout this book.

Parenting from the passenger seat is a metaphor for our role in honoring our children as the drivers of their own lives and our individual and collective responsibility for supporting them as they learn to trust their inner navigational compass—their conscience. Our children don't need more instruction; they need experience and connection to the broader world of possibilities. By pursuing meaningful endeavors with people, places, practices, and ideas, they learn who they are and how they can contribute. The personal and professional relationships they develop will help them find new opportunities in today's rapidly evolving economy.

Honoring the dignity of their individuality, we can ride alongside them as they learn to navigate life on their own and build critical networks of support. Recognizing the reality of our dependence on the education system and the current social construct, we can begin to build a bridge to community ecosystems of support while our children are still in the traditional schooling model. Together, our choices and actions can create environments that promote human flourishing. These environments will inspire our children to move forward in life with meaningful purpose and responsibility, knowing their uniqueness is invaluable to their community.

No two people are exactly alike, and we each have a different context to our lives. Therefore, we have different perspectives. I am sharing my perspective based on the context of my life so we can begin the discussion and debate about how we are raising children in our society. There is no perfect parent. We are all fallible human beings. We have much to learn from each other and our children. Because we share a common humanity and a desire for the well-being of all children, there are critical questions that we must answer together. Who is responsible for educating children? What role do children play in their own education? If they can't challenge concepts and ideas, can they really think critically and become the independent decision-makers our society needs? If they are not engaging with the real world while in school, are they genuinely being educated as future citizens and contributors?

This book is not about school reform, nor is it advocating for a certain type of public, private, charter, or homeschool. It is also not a book about how to parent your individual child. Every child is different, and so is every parent. My focus relates to the societal norms and conditions that affect how children are nurtured and families are supported within our communities. I am challenging the disconnected way we live, the meaningless approach to learning, and the central role industrialized schooling now plays in most children's lives. I am advocating for a realignment of responsibility for raising children from our current reliance on education systems to one where parents and communities support each other and encourage children to become the drivers of their own lives. Every person in our community can be a ripple contributing to a wave of change. I hope this book inspires you to join in.

———

Note: The term *parent* applies to any caregiver responsible for children, and the term *college* applies to both colleges and universities.

PART I

WHERE WE ARE

CHAPTER 1

WHAT ARE WE PREPARING OUR CHILDREN FOR?

Abundance of knowledge does not teach men to be wise.

—Heraclitus

"Mom, you don't know me!"

This was my wake-up call.

I had been walking by my then 14-year-old daughter's desk and noticed that she was on social media instead of finishing the homework she said she needed to complete. Although I was apprehensive about the role of school in her life, I knew she needed to focus on academics during high school to get into college. I wanted to talk with her about how I thought she should spend her time, and she had other ideas. Her hand was up like a stop sign as we stood glaring at each other.

Her comment took me off guard. I tried to wrap my head around what she was saying. True, we were both in uncharted territory. I had never been the mother of a teenager, and she was learning what it was like to be a teenager. Still, how could she say I didn't know her? She was the child I nursed and cared for. I knew what she did every day. My mind was screaming, *Of course I know you! I birthed you! I also know the world—which you don't.*

As the voice in my head kept rambling on, something deep down inside me registered with what she was saying. She was right. We can never really know someone else's experiences or how they interpret the world. She might have come through me, but she wasn't me. She couldn't have my same perspective; the context of her life was entirely different.

At that moment, I realized that my daughter Emily might be the physical manifestation of our family's genetics and the environment in which she was raised, but the essence of who she is—her human spirit or soul—belonged only to her. Of the 8 billion of us on this planet, not one of us is the same. This uniqueness makes each of us irreplaceable and essential to the interwoven fabric of life.

What was my role as her mother? Was it to mold and shape her to fit into society's image of success, or was it to support her in becoming the person she was meant to be—as defined by her? These are tricky questions in a society that judges parents on their children's academic and extracurricular achievements and whether or not they go to college. To be a good mother, I was supposed to strap my children to an academic conveyor belt and assume they would come out the other end as happy and financially secure adults.

Our cultural devotion to the preschool-to-college trajectory has become unquestioned and habitual. The future is unknown and unknowable, yet we absorb ourselves in some promised future outcome. We spend little time evaluating whether this trajectory actually works or even whether the life we are preparing them for will be a life well lived. With an eye toward purported future earnings, we ignore the significant cost of time, money, and more importantly, emotional well-being sacrificed along the way.

My daughter was right to stop me. She understood that she is not a static individual. Like all of us, she is in a never-ending process of becoming. She alone hears her conscience—her personal navigation system—and makes the necessary decisions about what to do in each situation she encounters. Her conscience is like a radar connected to some unknowable larger force. For some individuals, this force is God;

for others, it is the universe, creator, source, or higher power.

Although I can support them whenever possible, I cannot follow my children through their lives, making decisions and choices for them. Nor would I want to; it would deny them the ability to be themselves and contribute their uniqueness to the world. It would deprive them of the aliveness that comes with the agency and excitement of deciding which of all possibilities they are faced with that they will bring into reality. As Neale Donald Walsch says, "*Life begins at the end of your comfort zone.*"

Unique human beings do not live life in a linear manner. There is no pathway that our children need to follow; they are the path. They co-create the path as they engage with the world and with people, places, and ideas. We do not live separately from the world around us, and the co-creation process includes the contributions we make to the collective together with others and nature, which, in turn, contributes to who we are and influences our choices. We are meant to co-create our lives as part of an open ecosystem of engagement and to decide how we respond—using our free will—to the circumstances we find ourselves in.

THE SEPARATION FROM REAL-WORLD EXPERIENCES

How are our children supposed to co-create their lives when they are raised in closed systems? As our society has doubled down on testing and focused on college-for-all, fewer learners get exposed to real-world experiences alongside adults during their schooling. Worse, not all college learners gain exposure to their field through internships while doing their coursework. For 18 to 22 years, we put them all into an intellectual, theoretical simulator filled with our past understandings (from a single perspective). Then, at the end of their schooling, we turn them loose to figure out how to build a life—alone.

Kids are bored in school. The entire institutional structure of the

19

school system was built for a different era. Its content aligns more with teaching about the rotary phone than the smartphone. It is little wonder that student engagement decreases as they progress through school, from 75% in fifth grade to 32% by eleventh grade.[1] Sadly, a Gallup study showed that only 20% of workers are thriving in the workplace, even with low unemployment.[2] What exactly are we preparing our children for?

We need to recognize that academic knowledge does not generally translate to life skills and that the school simulator is almost completely disconnected from what real life looks like. Life does not have fixed answers, isolated subjects, batched age groups, or routine shifts at specific intervals. These are remnants of the factory model upon which our schools were built. They were designed for the compliance of factory workers—and now digital workers—and have not kept up with technological and economic transformations. **There is no way teachers, administrators, testing companies, or even policymakers can stay abreast of the content needed.**

Our approach to mass-producing education treats students like commodities to be shaped and molded along an assembly line. This prioritization of compliance and conformity has had huge ramifications for all of us as it has devalued diversity of all types—race, religion, intelligence, ideas, expression, etc. Our culture of sameness runs counter to the independent decision-making we hope our children learn and instead teaches them to be validated by external measures (grades, test scores, likes, followers, and so on).

The constant academic and extracurricular competition fuels isolation, meaninglessness, and social disconnection. These are key factors in the epidemic of mental illness we see today. Humans are not made to be separated from one another; we depend on each other for survival from the moment we are born. The framework of competition and comparison also turns teachers into judges and juries of the worthiness of individuality rather than empowerers of possibility and responsibility. Many opportunities in the transforming economy require self-direction, innovative thinking, and collaboration. Where will our children gain these skills?

Ironically, I often use the Department of Motor Vehicles (DMV) as an example of what needs to happen in education. There are many parallels between the two standardized systems, including reducing humans to numbers, ignoring individual circumstances, applying an assembly-line approach to the people using their mandatory services, and requiring memorization of content that is often forgotten in the real world. (Do you honestly remember how far away you can park from a fire hydrant if the curb isn't painted to remind you?)

But there is one critical difference that sets the DMV apart in applied learning that highlights a gaping hole in our education system: the DMV requires young people to drive with an adult for at least six months before going it alone. This difference is significant because it recognizes the clear distinction between book rules and road rules. It is the unwritten road rules that make us good drivers, and these rules are only learned through practice and experience. Seasoned adults play a vital role in riding alongside young drivers as they gain the under-standing they need to become competent.

Our children need the time and freedom to develop the kinds of meaningful mentoring and coaching relationships necessary for life and work. According to a LinkedIn survey and other similar studies, 85% of jobs are found through relationships.[3] Additionally, 70% of all jobs are not posted[4]—they are found only through personal and professional relationships. If most jobs are not posted, then how can it be determined that people need a college degree to get a well-paying job? The numbers are likely skewed by large corporate postings since word-of-mouth jobs are not easily tracked.

Regardless of their initial job, sooner rather than later, our children will need to look for new work and continue doing so throughout their lives. Full-time work does not offer the longevity it once did;

the average length of full-time employment for all age groups is 4.1 years and 2.8 years for those aged 25 to 34.[5] Additionally, freelance or independent work is growing at three times the rate of traditional employment,[6] creating a new type of economy. These factors are reshaping how we earn our living.

The strong focus on preparing students for a career in our current economy is like building a foundation on quicksand. The economy is shifting too fast. Although they will have to determine an initial focus to find work, they need to understand that the direction they move in will unfold as they go along. In reality, they need more than a job, they need a community. **We must prepare our children for continual life and work transitions.** Building communal and relational support can relieve some of the isolation and fear associated with finding new work. Learning to develop these capabilities and create supportive relationships starts when children are young, not when they graduate from school.

THE VALUE OF PERFORMANCE

Our society's mechanistic approach to raising children, with its performance-based value system, can be reflected in any type of schooling. It does not matter if it is public, private, charter, or homeschool. It manifests itself in the promotion of test scores, grade point averages (GPAs), college admissions (not completions), and most importantly, the emphasis on being a "good student."

We revere a young person who is a good student, especially one who achieves all A's in a broad spectrum of subjects. I question whether this is actually best for the student as it trains them to be expert conformists. They must ignore their intuitive guidance, individuality, and curiosities to adhere to societal measurements of worthiness. The overwhelming amount of work required to be a good student across all subjects leaves little time for pursuing meaningful interests, nurturing important relationships, or building communal networks of support.

I remember listening to the valedictorian's speech at one of my daughters' graduations and her sad lament about her lack of friends during her school experience. Although she had a long list of achievements, she regretted devoting so much time to studying rather than engaging in social interactions. After college applications were completed, she said she made an effort to develop friendships that then benefited her life tremendously.

Interestingly, few valedictorians end up as entrepreneurs.[7] They usually enter familiar hierarchical structures like corporations or institutions after graduation. Sadly, with these structures undergoing rapid transformation due to technological and global shifts, job stability can be continually undermined. Arguably, entrepreneurial skills are essential during rapidly changing times as they promote agility, creativity, mistakes, gut instincts, collaboration, and other beneficial qualities necessary for navigating life.

Even though it is impossible to compare one unique human being to another, we use "averages" as baselines for the comparison of students. The work of Todd Rose, author of *The End of Average: Unlocking Our Potential by Embracing What Makes Us Different* and the former director of Harvard's Mind, Brain, and Education Program, has shown that averaging human beings is scientifically and morally wrong.[8] Humans can't be averaged like widgets; we are too unique and have a multitude of immeasurable variables that affect us at any given moment. Measuring, averaging, and comparing individuals has created inaccurate perceptions and inequitable opportunities. How can we talk about "learning loss" or "not being at grade level" when these ideas are based on a mythical average human?

We have built an entire education system on this faulty premise. Grades, which are primarily subjective judgments composed of test scores, class assignments, and homework, compare each student to an average student at their grade level. The grade level is determined by where the average child is developmentally supposed to be at a certain age—even though there is no such thing as an average child! We have shamed millions of children through generations into believing they are not smart if their development doesn't adhere to the average. How sad is that?

If we really start to think about it, defining our children by school performance, and grades in particular, says nothing about them— their unique gifts, interests, or whether they matter to us. Academic performance really says that they have complied and conformed well to the standardized curriculum and that they have stayed in the competition—increasing envy, shame, and perfectionism. What has this cost them emotionally, physically, financially? What have our families, communities, and societies lost in their unrealized potential?

If students don't measure up to this sameness as defined by standardized tests, they are considered "off track." Ironically, many children labeled by the school system with "learning disabilities" like dyslexia and autism are later valued in the workplace.[9] Those with dyslexia see things in nontraditional ways, and many become entrepreneurs.[10] Students with autism are sought after in the tech world because of their ability to hyperfocus. In reality, all human beings are differently abled.

Our children are born into the world as unique beings, but they learn that their uniqueness is not valued. They must learn the same thing, at the same age, in the same amount of time, in the same way, in the same environment, and with the same goal: college admissions. But trying to distinguish themselves in this pool of sameness has been futile and exhausting. Over the past few decades, college access has expanded via student loan programs, the Common App, and global exposure through the internet. At the same time, vocational training and all other forms of workplace preparation fell out of favor because making money in a professional white-collar career is now the definitive status symbol. With a captive audience and demand on the rise, colleges began prioritizing applications based on quantifiable measurements. As a result, all students have been forced to use the same playbook to increase their grades and test scores, thereby increasing the pressure and competition.

I remember attending high school parent meetings related to college admissions. I soon understood that it didn't really matter about my child; it was all about the numbers—test scores and GPAs. There is no secret formula for getting students into the college of their choice. With an acceptance rate of less than 5%, thousands of valedictorians will not get into Harvard.

Meritocracy is a lie. Except for those few with special athletic abilities or artistic talents or those who have well-resourced parents with special connections, the ones who get in are *indistinguishable* from the ones who don't. Yet our children feel ashamed when they don't get accepted into the college of their choice—if college is an option at all. The ones who go to community college, trade schools, or into the workforce often feel like failures.

Our humanness is challenged by the factory-style education system. The foster youth trying to process a traumatic experience is expected to perform the same as the student whose family can provide academic and emotional support. All students are expected to progress along a linear path—from preschool to elementary school to middle school to high school to college—even though life isn't linear. It is not possible to make all humans the same—and why would we want to?

We often equate well-being with whether or not a student is doing well in school. We view anything related to education as inherently good. If it is in the name of education, we acquiesce to its demands and ignore the toll it is taking on our children, ourselves, and our communities. **We are blind to the fact that our standardized education system has become the master, not the servant.**

The lines between home and school life are no longer distinct. Since academic accomplishments have become a cultural reflection of parenting success, many families are over-involved and hyper-focused on outcomes. With internet access to grades and test scores, homework and activities can be monitored around the clock to ensure the priority stays on school. In this way, we reinforce that our children's value is tied to their academic performance, not to who they are as a person.

Child labor laws protect children from being exploited in the workplace, yet we think nothing of asking them to give up nights, weekends, vacations, and vital sleep in the name of education. In fact, we honor and *reward* them for doing so. The constant pressure to perform at optimal mental levels is exacting a terrible toll on our children.

As long as we focus on preparing children to fit into industrialized systems, we will continue to define them as not measuring up or call them "learning disabled" based on their inability to learn the standardized curriculum within specified time constraints. We even medicate them when they don't conform well to the protocols. **We need to stop asking, "*how smart is my child?*" based on academic standards and instead start asking, "*how is my child smart?*"**

During the COVID-19 pandemic lockdown, all three of my daughters came home. They were 19, 20, and 22 at the time. My youngest, Allison, was especially bored. I asked her what she would do if she were in a room where she could learn anything she wanted. She immediately responded that she would love to learn to sew and design her own clothes. We drove to my mom's house and borrowed her 30-year-old sewing machine and some leftover fabric. Allison set herself up on the dining room table with YouTube and taught herself how to sew. She was not interested in buying patterns; she wanted to make her own. With trial and error and an aptitude for math, she made some really nice outfits.

It was a joy to watch my daughter enter a flow state with sewing. She loved learning all about fashion design. We went to a fabric store when things opened back up, and she was so happy pulling out bolts of fabric and imagining what she would make. When it came time to return to her college, she realized it didn't have a major related to fashion. I suggested she start a website with a few designs and see where it went, but she felt she needed to be properly trained in a large company. (Even though both her parents are entrepreneurs, she has been programmed to believe that she needed to follow an established step-by-step progression.) She liked her digital media major enough and her friends even more, so she remained at her school. Although she didn't think anything of it, I often wonder what would have happened if she had discovered her interest in sewing a lot earlier.

COLLEGE-FOR-ALL

The meteoric rise in the cost of college, the devaluing of degrees by businesses, and the demand for skills-based talent have begun to challenge our college-for-all narrative. The massive institutional failure going on for decades is becoming more apparent. Out of necessity, companies are increasingly recognizing the huge untapped pool of candidates available without a college degree. The availability of short-term skills training, increased apprenticeships for traditional and technical trades, and the escalating value of hands-on experience are all transforming the character of the workforce.

Unfortunately, many students have ended up in a generation caught between two worlds—the degree-valuing corporate hierarchical model of yesteryear and the project-based technical and trade skills required in today's world. The agility needed to navigate the transition is not something our children have learned well. It is not their fault, but it is their reality.

If we take a closer look at our economy, more than seven out of ten jobs (7 out of 10!)[11] do not require a Bachelor's Degree. Demand is so strong in many non-degree fields—trades, technology, construction—

that they are well-paying. The cost of training for these programs is much lower and often paid. Skilled tradespeople are very smart in math and science as they routinely apply the principles in their work; they just don't refer to them by memorized formulas. When the cost of time and money is factored in, actual earnings are higher in many of these fields than those requiring degrees.

Yet, we still cling to the illusion that our children will be prepared for life and gainfully employed throughout their lives if they follow the prescribed path to college. Many parents say they want them to have a degree "to fall back on" if they ever need it. This is a risky proposition. While a college degree has worked for some, it has not worked for the *vast majority*.

Our education system is a leaky funnel. Of every 100 high school students entering ninth grade, only 28 will graduate with a degree (within 6 years).[12] Further, of those recent graduates, only 16 will get a job that requires a degree.[13] No business could continue to operate with this dismal return on investment.

For many reasons, it is difficult for most students to follow the rigid protocols required to complete their degrees in a six-year period (National Center for Education Statistics, NCES, doesn't quote four-year information, which is even lower). Mainstream media are finally highlighting the reality of the time required. A November 2021 article in *Forbes* titled "Shocking Statistics About College Graduation Rates" notes:

> *Even after six years, less than 60% of students at four-year colleges have earned a Bachelor's Degree. The track record for community colleges is even worse, with less than 20% of community college students earning an Associate's Degree or Certificate.*[14]

Having more graduates with degrees doesn't generate more jobs requiring degrees. Our consumer-driven economy determines the types of jobs needed and the wages given. Although most students attend college to get well-paying jobs, many of those jobs do not pay a wage that covers the graduate's expenses. It depends largely on the chosen field, the geographic location, and the length of time required to earn the degree.

The added time to get a degree today can substantially increase the overall expense. Additionally, those who drop out—as a large number do—still have the debt obligation. The burden of student loans is significant for young people and can affect their life choices and opportunities. **If college delivered a higher earnings guarantee, why did the Biden Administration repeatedly call for U.S. taxpayers to forgive or relieve over $400 billion in student loan debt because of the financial hardship it created for so many?**

Colleges need to be more accountable for whether their degrees and tuition prices produce the promised financial return. Their business model favors higher socio-economic groups, but the return on investment of time and money is not always justified. My daughter, a speech therapist with a good job, would not have financial stability if she'd had to take out significant loans to pay for her education. My other two daughters have chosen creative fields, which are notoriously low paying. Our societal promise that a degree will pay off is like telling our children to take out a $100,000 loan to buy a $50,000 house. They won't have enough money to furnish it or to enjoy an evening out, but they will have a home—which is really owned by the bank. It is truly absurd!

I am not suggesting that a college degree doesn't deliver promised benefits to some students. Those with minimal debt and degrees in high-demand fields like engineering can do very well. It has just not worked out as a successful formula for most students, even though it is routinely touted as producing guaranteed lifelong income for *all* who attain a degree. How do they determine lifelong income in such a rapidly transforming economy where the duration of most jobs is only a few years?

I'm reminded of what happened with taxi medallions, the operating permits controlling the number of taxis allowed in one city. In New York, at its peak, these medallions cost upward of $1 million and were highly prized.[15] Within a short time, ride-for-hire services like Uber and Lyft significantly diminished their value and left medallion owners without the benefit of their sizable investment. The value of college credentials is currently undergoing a similar upheaval.

Assuming a college degree will benefit everyone follows the same illogical thinking we use to average human beings. The pay for jobs requiring a degree varies *significantly* depending on the field chosen. Not all students will be interested in pursuing an engineering, medical, or legal degree—some of the highest-earning fields that require a college degree. Those wishing to be in a creative field or social services will be paid considerably less. Forcing students into jobs they are not interested in because of status or promised earnings usually doesn't work out well in the long run. The inauthenticity of this life can eventually result in mental, emotional, or physical ailments.

The issue of gaining real-world experience through internships has its own built-in challenges and inequities. Many are unpaid, which affects the ability of students to earn money while they are going to school. Sometimes internships are used for class credit, so the college is paid for the opportunity. Internships are essential for gaining the work experience many companies require today as well as securing entry-level employment after graduation. However, on some college campuses, the inability to sublease housing can limit accessibility to internships for specific field opportunities and geographic locations. Ultimately, internships tend to favor well-resourced students.

When emotional and financial costs are factored in, college may not be the most beneficial path for all students, especially going straight there after high school. Some argue that it helps prepare good citizens, but in looking around at the society that has evolved during our singular push for everyone to go through institutional preparation, it's clear that these desired results have yet to appear. We are as divisive as ever.

The concept of college-for-all is based on an outmoded paradigm that never applied to most people in the first place. We no longer live a three-part life—school until age 25, work until age 65, then retirement. The reality today is that we must continually upskill and reskill throughout our lives to keep up with technological changes. The wonderful thing is that a college degree, if needed or desired, can be obtained at any point in life. Regardless of the reality, we still hang on to this strong cultural narrative. Why? Because we wish it were true. Every parent wants to be able to guarantee that their child will have a successful adult life.

By focusing on earnings as the goal of a college degree, we ignore the costly price we have all paid to the quality of our lives in the present, especially for children. The loss of time for play and exploration throughout their early years and the mental distress created by never-ending demands often have lifelong implications. What would the world be like if we focused on preparing our children to live a meaningful life instead of having them spend their childhoods checking the boxes to enter college?

A SOCIETY OF INSTITUTIONAL SYSTEMS

Over the past half-century, we have turned over our individual and collective responsibility for raising children to public and private education systems. These highly bureaucratic systems now dictate the rhythm of life in most of our homes. Our daily lives are consumed with the exhausting and overwhelming grind of keeping ourselves and our children on task.

We are continually modeling this lifestyle to our children as we push them faster and faster on the one-size-fits-all education hamster wheel. When we orchestrate their every move with adult-directed activities, we leave little time for them to explore their interests, nurture relationships, or learn to make their own decisions. They are forced to remain passengers rather than drivers of their own lives. In complying with authority figures or conforming to peers, they learn to suppress their intuitive guidance and the decision-making ability needed to navigate their own way. Is this truly how we want them to live life?

In reality, we are preparing our children to enter a society of systems. These institutional systems feed other systems and support multi-industrial business interests; they do not nurture human beings or promote thriving communities. Whether it is the education system, healthcare system, foster care system, criminal justice system, agriculture system, governmental system, or corporate system, our dependence on these institutions rather than communities has made them tyrannical dictators of our lives. We are answerable to their demands and processes and have ended up being treated like commodities rather than people. This has proven unhealthy for individuals both inside and outside of the systems.

These systems have a role to play in our society, but we have overburdened them with a level of responsibility unsuitable to their abilities. Those members of our society without the resources to go outside the systems are especially susceptible to their failure and the inequities they have produced. By virtue of their massive form, hierarchical structure, and transactional approach, these systems cannot meet our human needs. Sadly, caring individuals working within these institutions are often caught in standardized accountability measures that limit time for individualized attention.

Productivity and *efficiency* are industrial terms, not human terms. Rather than working a job as a means to an end to provide for our families or to honor a professional calling, we have become the means to an end for measurable institutional or organizational outputs. In many cases, we are not asked to contribute our unique selves to the mission at hand. Instead, we are identified by the titles, categories, or roles deemed necessary to achieve predetermined institutional goals. We've become conduits through which organizations filter top-down dictates to achieve desired results. In the workplace, we are discarded when our usefulness is no longer needed—something that happens regularly as technology advances.

The burnout epidemic in teachers, principals, social workers, psychologists, doctors, nurses, office workers, parents, and more reflects the challenges created by the mechanistic way we live and the failure of these institutional systems. Although many view this as a problem of the individual, it is ultimately a societal issue. **How have we evolved to value numeric, financial, or shareholder returns more than the human stakeholders who provide the day-to-day results?**

Education is a powerful tool for humanity's advancement. True education happens everywhere and is ongoing. Human beings are born to learn. We learn about ideas, relationships, places, and things through engagement and experiences. Perhaps our misstep has been equating education with school. Academic knowledge is considered the pinnacle of achievement today, but this singularity has limited our children's exposure to the wide variety of experiences and relationships that can educate them as whole human beings. How ironic is it that our devotion to academic learning could limit our children's thinking and the possibilities available to them in the transforming world?

We need a diversity of intelligences to strengthen our society. Do we really want to prioritize only intellectual brainiacs—which is impossible anyway since people cannot be programmed like robots— over caregivers, skilled tradespeople, and artists? What a bleak society! It is also one that does not function well. The COVID-19 pandemic highlighted the definition of an "essential" worker to all of us.

Attempting to mass produce a specific type of intellectual smartness in all children has been a disaster. Decades ago, astronomer Carl Sagan noticed this exact problem when talking with young people:

> My experience is, you go talk to kindergartners or first-grade kids, you find a class full of science enthusiasts.
>
> And they ask deep questions. They ask, "What is a dream, why do we have toes, why is the moon round, what is the birthday of the world, why is grass green?"
>
> These are profound, important questions. They just bubble right out of them.
>
> You go talk to 12th grader students and there's none of that. They've become leaden and incurious. Something terrible has happened between kindergarten and 12th grade and it's not just puberty.

Sagan's observations are supported by studies that show capacities for creativity decline as children move through the school system. In a landmark study conducted by George Land, 5-year-old kindergarten students scored 98% in creativity.[16] At age 10, these same children scored 30%, and at age 15, they scored 12%. By the time they were adults, they were at 2% creative capacity. In today's economy, creativity is considered one of the top skills necessary for success in the workplace.

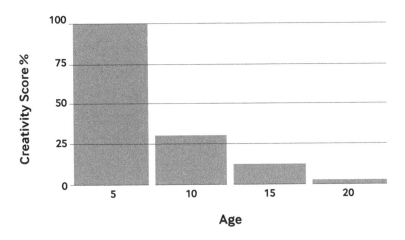

We rely on the education system to ready students for life and work, but it creates simulations that bear no resemblance to the real world. By virtue of its bureaucratic structure, it cannot honor individuality, nor can it infuse the agility necessary for living life. It has proven inadequate in preparing our children to navigate their own way as adults with dignity and belonging and to take advantage of emerging industries and opportunities. Amid massive institutional failure, we still cling to its authority as the purveyors of our children's future.

The faster we run on the treadmill of modern life, the more disconnected we have become from ourselves, each other, nature, and meaningful pursuits. The constant comparison to others, the encouragement of competition for rankings and external prizes, and the hyperfocus on a single definition of success (equating to wealth and status) have all contributed to feelings of isolation, meaninglessness, and loneliness. These, in turn, have fueled an epidemic of anxiety, depression, aggression, addiction, and suicide.

PREPARATION FOR HUMAN FLOURISHING

New opportunities can emerge if we focus on human-centered rather than organization-centered frameworks. Our systems can return to the function they were originally intended to perform: tools we humans use when we need them. Their size, authority, and reach must be balanced with personal and community responsibility for the care and support of each other. The financial and emotional instability in many homes necessitates the building of human support networks in local communities, not industrialized systems. We must honor the dignity of individuals and reintegrate the separated generations to ensure health and well-being for all.

It sounds like a huge undertaking, but humans have done it throughout the ages. It just takes a few to get it started, and change will begin. Many people are in survival mode and need this societal change to be able to breathe. For their sake and our own, we each must do what we can to contribute to the shift.

The Great Resignation and the surge in alternative schooling choices following the COVID-19 pandemic accelerated a growing movement toward taking back our humanness and restoring community support. The defiant power of the human spirit is alive and well. The future is what we all create, including our children. Every person has an essential role to play. The ecosystems that encourage human flourishing involve interconnectedness in communities rather than mechanical systems. A standardized curriculum will not prepare our children for a meaningful future—that needs to be determined by them.

Regardless of our work, resilience and life satisfaction rest on relationships as we move through our lives. This is true for all age groups. One of the longest-running studies conducted over 80 years by Harvard determined that *"close relationships, more than money or fame, are what keep people happy throughout their lives."*[17] We must prepare our children for a life that prioritizes the people and experiences that make life worth living.

Old systems break down before new ones are fully formed, and right now we find ourselves in this in-between place. We are all working hard to redefine how we live, learn, work, and play. Technology, which fueled our dramatic economic transformation, can provide the tools we need to shift the paradigm.

This transformation we are undergoing creates an opportunity to reassess our value systems and reimagine the future. Working together, we must build new educational and social infrastructure that responds to the needs of our children's human qualities while preparing them to make continual decisions throughout their lives that will affect them *and* their communities. Education should not leave our children with lifelong mental, physical, or financial burdens. We need a communal ecosystem of multigenerational relationships and expansive learning environments that reflect the unique situations, interests, and paths of each child.

We are the gatekeepers of our children's possibilities. What are we preparing them for? Rather than preparing them for system dependence, we can prepare them to know they are meant to be in this world and that they have a responsibility to contribute in whatever way is right for *them*. We can prepare them to LIVE rather than merely exist, to feel alive as they navigate the uncertainty inherent in life. They can become the drivers of their own lives if we prepare them to make meaningful decisions, listen to their inner navigator, and change the world by continually transforming themselves.

———

CHAPTER 2

WHAT IN THE NAME OF EDUCATION ARE WE DOING?

An abnormal reaction to an abnormal situation is normal behavior.

—Viktor Frankl

The world has dramatically changed. Our children know it. The material they are required to process is often irrelevant and unrelatable, yet they must devote hours at school *and at home* to memorizing it. They are rarely allowed outside to engage freely with the real world. We wonder what has happened to their mental health, but if we look closer, we should not be surprised by their reaction. They are anxious because they don't feel they can measure up to all the expectations around them and are suffocating from the confinement. They are exhausted from trying to keep up with both the mounds of content and their peers. They are deflated from feeling like their value is only in their external performance—one that can be quantified and measured.

Student suicide attempts and hospitalizations mirror the school calendar.[1] Suicide is now a leading cause of death among teenagers, and it is on the rise.[2] Frightening statistics are reported regularly, and it is not uncommon now to hear of someone from my own community who has taken their life. Today, suicide is the *second* leading cause of death in children ages 10 to 14, which is fifth through ninth grade![3] Why are we ignoring this?

Most parents say they want their children to be happy. However, happiness will vary by individual and change with life's transitions and events. Happiness researcher Shawn Achor notes that ancient Greeks defined happiness as *"the joy we feel while striving for our potential."*[4] The reality is that happiness ensues from the **pursuit of meaning**.

Meaning is what makes us human and distinguishes us from other animals. It is our primary motivation for living and a key factor in mental health and well-being, according to Viktor Frankl, renowned psychiatrist and survivor of the Holocaust.[5] He developed an understanding of the critical role meaning plays in our lives through his extensive work with suicidal patients and his own experiences in concentration camps. When I learned about his life and work, with its deep reverence for our messy humanness and the responsibility we have for making the most of our lives, it provided clarity to my personal philosophy.

When asked to define *meaning*, Frankl would say, *"What is meant."*[6] The underlying concept of meaning is the fact that who we are and what we do matters to the world. We each have a unique and irreplaceable role to play in the fabric of life that relates to the unknowable, ultimate meaning of our existence. Meaning is specific to the individual and discovered by them. It cannot be given, invented, or created. Meaning refers to what is meant and intended specifically for each of us in the situations we are confronted with during our lives.

The recognition of meaning has a pulling effect toward certain possibilities. We are guided in our decision of how best to respond by our conscience (sometimes referred to as intuition or gut feeling). Meaning is connected to our values. We give meaning to our lives when we create or do something that contributes to the world or when we experience beauty (art, music, nature), truth, or the love of another person. Meaning can be found under all circumstances, including unavoidable circumstances like illness or the death of a loved one. In these situations, the stand or attitude we take can be meaningful.

Meaning varies from person to person and moment to moment.

It relates only to what resonates with that unique individual in the distinct situations and circumstances encountered in life. It is something we discover through an inner knowing or the curiosity we feel when we see or experience something. Sometimes it is a vague sensation, and sometimes it pops out at us, and we have an "ah ha!" reaction. We have free will to choose whether or not to respond to the attention-grabbing possibility.

The discovery of meaning is not always related to positive situations. An emergency room doctor working tirelessly to save lives can find meaning in their work, even though the outcome is not always desirable. Frankl's research determined that happiness, joy, fulfillment, and success are not found through direct pursuit; they are the side effects of finding and fulfilling meaning.

For education to have meaning to our children, it must be driven individually by them rather than driven by the adults in their lives. It must relate to their interests and the causes that matter to them. It requires engagement and interaction with the world around them as they learn through trial and error, as all humans do. Since meaning plays a key role in mental health and well-being, our children must learn to follow their innate knowing and orient themselves toward meaningful pursuits, experiences, and attitudes.

MY SEARCH FOR MEANING

An acquaintance of mine, Margarita Solazzo, came up to me at an event to tell me that she talked about my blog to anyone who would listen. She was involved on hospital boards and with community mental health initiatives and was the mother of two young adult daughters. The issues I raised deeply resonated with her own experiences, and she told me, *"Once you see, you can't unsee."*

Margarita asked me if I was familiar with Viktor Frankl and his book, *Man's Search for Meaning*. I told her it was one of my favorite books. I was deeply impacted by his experiences in concentration camps and inspired by his hopeful message that meaning can be found under any condition. I, along with 16 million others who have read the book, am so appreciative of Frankl's deep commitment to those experiencing suffering and the resources that can be found in our spiritual dimension. Margarita's cousin in Spain had started the Viktor Frankl Institute in Valencia, and she came to know Frankl's grandson, Alexander "Alex" Vesely-Frankl, through that connection. To my surprise and delight, she told me that he was staying with her and wanted us to meet.

The next week, the three of us met for lunch. Alex and I immediately connected around our shared view about how the education system treats humans like programmable robots. In addition to his passion for filmmaking, Alex is trained in his grandfather's psychological theory, called Logotherapy (healing through meaning), and is the keeper of the family archives. I learned that Viktor Frankl had similar concerns about our mechanistic and reductionist approach to students (and all humans, for that matter). Following our lunch, Alex shared with me some archived video clips and articles of Viktor Frankl talking about education. Using the resources he provided, I wrote "The Real Cost of a Meaningless Education." It became my most viewed blog post.

This is where my life took a very unexpected turn. After the blog was published, Alex wanted me to meet the producers he had partnered with for the feature film of *Man's Search for Meaning*. They were interested in doing a short documentary about youth suicide, but the idea of meeting Hollywood producers did not sound appealing to me at all. As a parent, I was not a fan of Hollywood and the content it produced. I rarely watched movies or TV and did my best to limit my children's exposure—until streaming platforms accessible on their phones and laptops made it impossible to control.

At Alex's insistence, I agreed to meet with Kate Cohen and

Marisa Polvino of Straight Up Films, one of the few women-owned production companies. We met in San Diego in an apartment building conference room next to Rady Children's Hospital, where Kate's then 7-year-old son was undergoing cancer treatment. Margarita and Straight Up Films Creative Director Katie Menke joined as well. Our meeting lasted for six hours, and I knew I had found my people. Kate, Marisa, and Katie were moms who were equally concerned about the rise in mental illnesses and suicides in young people. We all wanted to do something about it.

Never say never. I said I would never be involved with Hollywood, yet the inspiring collaboration that started in that tiny conference room led to my co-founding a new film company with Kate and Marisa called Straight Up Impact. Our first project together was a short documentary series with the working title *Meaning in Madness* to reflect the critical role meaning plays in our lives and our cultural madness in ignoring it.

The series emerged from a question and a quote. We asked ourselves, *"Why are so many children plagued by anxiety, depression, addiction, and worst of all, suicide?"* Reflecting on Viktor Frankl's quote about abnormal reactions to abnormal situations, we wondered whether the abnormal reactions children are exhibiting are actually normal given the situations we are placing them in.

Each episode in the ongoing series highlights the personal stories of youth impacted by our industrial and digital systems. To date, we have completed three, related to education, healthcare (overprescribing medications to kids), and foster care. Miraculously, we found inspiring youth who were willing to tell their stories for each episode. This was not easy, as we had to identify someone with a personal story they wanted to share, who would be comfortable on camera, and most of all, whose parents permitted them to share it. Whenever possible, the parents themselves are included in the films to provide additional context, as are various industry professionals.

Meeting these amazing young people and listening to them bravely share their perspectives keeps our team motivated to bring these important stories to a wide audience. Future episodes will highlight other systemic, digital, and cultural impacts on youth mental health and wellness, including the juvenile justice system, agricultural system, news media, body dysmorphia, violent video games, and more.

My involvement in film led me to co-found additional ventures, including the Viktor Frankl Institute of America (with Alex and Moira), to bring Frankl's meaning-oriented philosophy to modern U.S. audiences and B-Unbound,[7] which I will describe in later chapters. I also became an executive producer on the forthcoming feature film of *Man's Search for Meaning*. I studied Logotherapy through Frankl's writings and have been fortunate to have Alex as my mentor. I am not interested in becoming a clinical therapist, but I believe the principles Frankl advocated for—dignity, freedom, responsibility, and love—can be helpful to everyone.

I have no idea where these new ventures will lead, but they are meaningful endeavors that have energized this stage of my life. I am following the bouncing ball and responding to what shows up rather than directing where I am going. I am embracing the uncertainty and enjoying my collaborations with the amazing people who have come into my life. All the ventures I am currently involved with seemed to be independent at the time they were started, but looking back and connecting the dots, they all relate to my strong desire to advocate for voiceless young people.

Bryan Jacobson, my jokester brother-in-law, was searching the internet to find evidence that an alien ship had landed in Northern California on the day I was born. He thought this would be funny to include in my birthday card. Instead, he found out that on my birthday, November 20, 1959, the Declaration of the Rights of the Child (Resolution 1386) was unanimously adopted by the seventy-eight member states of the United Nations General Assembly. In summary, this declaration says that *"the child is recognized universally as a human being who must be able to develop physically, mentally, morally, spiritually, and socially . . . in conditions of freedom and dignity."*[8]

The two-page declaration detailing the rights of the child and the responsibilities of parents and community members to ensure their safety and protection resonates strongly with me and fuels my mission. The spirit of this resolution has not been honored, and we must remedy that. The opportunities for sustainable change and healing can be found in our communities, with each one of us contributing what we can from where we are. Our individual contributions, added to the collective, can shift our societal trajectory.

THE RESPONSIBILITY OF SCHOOLS

Although we rely on them, schools are not physically, organizationally, or financially set up to handle all that needs to be done to support students and prepare them for life. Educators are spread thin, implementing programs unrelated to their educational mission. The burden of solving all our children's ills—from hunger to mental health— has now been unfairly placed on schools because that is where children are contained. They are also our society's primary providers of childcare. **Schools are designed for the benefit of adults, not children.**

Teachers have taken the brunt of the massive institutional failure we are experiencing because they are the face of the system. Even though many of them disapprove, a teacher's time must be spent preparing for the quantitative measurements that determine their students' cultural acceptance and their job security. Most enter the field with a love of learning and a dedication to children, yet the demands from both the bureaucracy and parents have led to burnout and high turnover.

As we have passed on parenting responsibilities to schools, our home lives have begun to mirror the transactional character of these institutional relationships. Our short time together with our children revolves around questions like "Did you do your homework?" or "What time is the game?" or "How was the test?" The focus is on productive output, not the person. We are not conveying that we truly see them.

We live in a paternalistic society with a "father knows best" approach to governance that provides for people's needs without giving them rights and responsibilities. We require children to unquestioningly follow what parents and schools say they need to do. They must fit a specific mold rather than belong as they are with all their complex humanness. We assume that education will lead to a good, well-paying job, and they will be happy someday, ignoring the loss of the present, irretrievable moment. As discussed in the first chapter, this assumption that education leads to well-paying work and financial benefits for all has been challenged by the increased cost of college and our transforming economy.

Some people believe that sending children to school keeps them safe from abusive homes or neighborhoods, but this is not always the case. Unfortunately, emotional and physical abuse from peers and adults can happen in schools as well. Bullying in all its forms, including on social media, is a discharge of pain, and it dramatically impacts student well-being. It is difficult for overburdened school administrators to address these concerns if they even find out about them.

The school environment can also elicit feelings of shame and inadequacy with the pressure of tests, homework, and competitive activities such as sports. Even though some children can do well in the classroom, written and timed tests can give them anxiety and impact their performance. In addition, not everyone expresses themselves well through writing. Some express themselves best through movement, voice, art, music, or building things with their hands—things that can't really be measured. There is no way to create a one-size-fits-all learning environment that is equitable for all students.

The fencing surrounding many playgrounds and schools reminds me of a cage. Our children are confined to physical spaces, disconnected from nature, and stuck within rigid bureaucratic frameworks that devalue their humanness. We argue about whether the cages we have placed them in are tin or gold but ignore that they are in cages. It is the framework of the system itself that must be addressed.

We've lost sight of the quality of our children's lives today and the essential role and responsibility they have to contribute their uniqueness to our society. They emerge from our system of schooling without an understanding of who they are, which can lead them to believe that they are the ones who are broken, not the system. This affects all races and socio-economic groups. Both neglect and over-attention produce the same outcomes for many children: an inability to function well in life and the need to escape the pain.

INTO THE VOID

The confinement of our human spirit within these systems is distressing for everyone involved, including students, teachers, administrators, and parents. We are meaning-oriented human beings, and the internal upheaval from our mechanistic lifestyle creates a void in us. Frankl called this meaningless void the "existential vacuum."[9] Through his medical practice and experiences, he determined that we react to this vacuum by filling it with *aggression* toward ourselves or others, *addiction* in order to numb, or *depression*, which can lead to despair and suicide.[10]

The hallmarks of meaninglessness are boredom (lack of interest) and apathy (lack of motivation). These are everywhere in our industrialized and digitized world. They happen in welfare states and capitalistic societies—anywhere that the dignity of the individual is denied or that we are reduced to nothing but a brain to be programmed or behavior to be trained.

We are an "I" not an "it."

It is common for students to be bored and apathetic. This reduction of our children to machine-like robots devalues the wholeness and complexity of being human. Frankl often quoted social philosopher William Irwin Thompson as saying, "*Humans are not objects that exist as tables and chairs. They live—and, if they find that their lives are reduced to the mere existence of chairs or tables, then they commit suicide.*"[11]

I used to tell my children that everyone carries around an energy pain ball. When pressure builds up, that energy gets discharged outward toward others or inward toward ourselves, sometimes both. Reactions to this existential vacuum are expressed through bullying, violence, eating disorders, cutting, illicit drug use, media binging, alcoholism, and more. Hurt people hurt people and themselves. We are a society in pain.

SOCIAL SILOS

The mental and physical confinement to programs, buildings, and sports fields has limited our children's worldviews and created social silos within our organizational frameworks. Rather than allowing them to spend time at multigenerational engagements out in the community, which could provide continuity throughout life transitions, we restrict their interactions outside the home to same-age cohorts and adults who are paid to coach or care for them.

Without understanding the critical role they are meant to play in the world or the power of independent decision-making, our children end up conforming to what others do, depending on authority figures to tell them what to do, or rebelling against it all. Their lives lack the context of experiences and relationships that would inform their decisions and provide them with a broad web of support.

Our children join organized activities and attend school, but when they age out of these intense and concentrated experiences, their social infrastructure is gone, and they are often adrift. This disconnection can lead to identifying with larger groups so they don't feel alone. The most extreme example of this would be gangs, which are notorious for providing the illusion of belonging that relational human beings need to avoid feeling isolated.

We seek this sense of belonging through affiliations with sports teams, schools, political parties, races, religions, and so on. But often, the zealous allegiance to these affiliations leads to labeling and characterizing all individuals within the group as one identity, resulting in lost individuality and deep societal divisions. How do we build communities where children can belong without losing their individuality?

Our modern social interconnectedness is situation-based, not community-based. Friendships with peers are disrupted by the continual shift in grade levels, teams, schools, or a move out of the community by families. These shifts also impact the social lives of parents, as we often rely on friendships formed with the parents of our children's classmates, teammates, and friends from other activities.

Relationships with teachers can provide momentary and vital lifelines for children, but teachers don't usually live with them or stay nearby throughout their lives. The relationships with wonderful, caring people who work in our school systems like teachers and coaches usually end when our children move to the next grade level or graduate.

The segmentation of our society into silos and the transactional nature of our institutional relationships have contributed to another factor affecting young people's (and everyone else's) mental and physical health: loneliness. U.S. Surgeon General Vivek Murthy defines loneliness as being different from isolation and solitude. *"Loneliness is a subjective feeling where the connections we need are greater than the connections we have. In the gap, we experience loneliness. It's distinct from the objective state of isolation, which is determined by the number of people around you."*[12]

It seems counterintuitive that with all their technical connectedness and constant participation in group activities, young people identify among the loneliest in our society.[13] Continuous competition and comparison make the deepening of true friendships complicated and further exacerbate feelings of loneliness. This is not only affecting young people, but other age groups as well, especially the elderly. Murthy noted that during his years as a doctor, the most common pathology he saw was *"not heart disease or diabetes; it was loneliness."*

Loneliness is a significant contributor to increased risk of anxiety, depression, heart disease, dementia, and shorter lifespans.[14] It also affects sleep, an essential factor in health and well-being. The resulting mental and physical distress from loneliness cannot be treated medically until it manifests into symptoms, and even then, authentic human-to-human connection is required for healing.

This view of the social silos in which we raise our children was really driven home to me by my daughter Rachel, who loves comedic acting and screenwriting. She was born funny and has always made our family laugh. When she was 18 and graduating high school, I suggested she just go out and try her hand at comedy. It would certainly cost less than a college degree, and the entertainment industry hires based on talent, not degrees. She understood that but said, *"Who am I going to hang out with, Mom?"*

That is when the lack of gathering places for young people within our communities hit me. There aren't town squares or regular communal engagements that encourage daily interactions. I understood what she meant. As humans, the idea of being isolated and alone is a frightening prospect. She wanted to go where her peers were going so she could be socially connected. She also wanted to be trained in a structured program and felt a degree gave her validity in life—something we had reinforced early on.

I am a mentor to young adults who find their way to me through friends or friends of friends and in the course of my volunteer work.

They come from a broad range of socio-economic backgrounds. They, along with my children, have taught me so much and continue to fuel my advocacy. They are each brilliant in their own way. Some are in high school, some have graduated college, some are working corporate jobs, and others are drifting through their days, trying to figure out what they want to do. The loneliness and feelings of meaninglessness they are all experiencing are palatable and heartbreaking.

Our children desperately want a sense of community and deep, authentic connection, but we have yet to provide them with environments that facilitate that type of engagement, nor have we given them a fundamental understanding of how they can create it themselves. Even those who find strong communal schools are often surprised by how alone they feel once they are out in the real world. Our social silos, the isolated ways we live in confined spaces, and the transactional nature of most relationships in our society have frustrated the search for meaning and fragmented our essential social infrastructure.

The experiences and relationships our children encounter inform them about themselves and the world, helping them decide which direction to take and when to pivot. Although they may step onto some collective pathways along the way, with the world ever-changing and with themselves always in the process of becoming, these pre-existing pathways will only suffice for a short time. Guided by their intuitive conscience, they must decide which choices to make at each moment. Even indecision is a decision that affects the direction of their lives.

Unfortunately, we have not taught children to listen to their intuition and make independent and authentic decisions. Instead, we force them to fit into factory-style systems where they are batched and sorted by age and treated like receptacles for information. Their adult-controlled environments are confining; they cannot challenge their teachers, go to the bathroom when they want, eat when hungry, or deeply explore their interests and curiosities. Our children are multi-dimensional, complex human beings, not widgets.

Here's the crux: Unique human beings—designed to engage with the world—don't fit well into closed systems. We have eyes that face outward and senses that inform us. Before mirrors or cameras, this is how we understood the world. We cannot be shaped to fit external values or prescribed measurements. This confinement runs counter to what we need to thrive, and it creates immense distress.

SEEING THE REFLECTION

Our children are a reflection of the health and well-being of our society. And many—dare I say most—are not well. They are screaming at us that they need help, but they are not using words. They are screaming at us with their anxiety, depression, addiction, and suicide rates. Their inner turmoil is reflected in their stomachaches, headaches, self-harming, and numbing mechanisms. Rather than looking at the context of their environment, we treat individual students as the problem and label or medicate them so they can progress through our standardized education system. What are we doing to our children in the name of education?

Loneliness and meaninglessness are social issues, not medical issues. For most of human history, individuals have been responsible for the care and well-being of each other. However, during the past century, our society has come to depend on institutional care as the first line of defense in addressing all medical, physical, and emotional issues. With six in ten U.S. adults suffering from chronic diseases,[15] the pressures on the healthcare system are unrelenting.

Adding to the demand for physical care is the escalating need for mental healthcare services. Given the finite number of psychiatrists and psychologists unevenly distributed throughout the country, the responsibility given to systemized mental healthcare is unsustainable.[16] Many areas do not even offer crisis intervention or mental healthcare services. The cost of higher education, the long timeframes required for certification, and the well-documented burnout of medical and psychiatric professionals further exacerbate the problem. We have come to depend on intervention rather than prevention. What if the way we are living in confined silos and relying on institutional systems is contributing to the mental health crisis in our youth?

Looking at this complex issue from a different perspective highlights an opportunity for relief. **We are relational human beings in a society that depends on transactional care**—even when delivered by committed professionals. Since the health and well-being of each individual in a community determines the health and well-being of the overall community, this is where we need to begin: together.

———

CHAPTER 3

WHAT'S LOVE GOT TO DO WITH IT?

Courage is not the absence of fear, but rather the assessment that
something else is more important than fear.

—Franklin D. Roosevelt

The idea of being responsible for how we truly show up in the world and honoring our children's individuality is scary. But love is greater than fear. We instinctively override our fears when our children are threatened. With a rush of adrenaline, we will run to intercede if they are being attacked by a dog or about to get hit by a car. We transform the energy of fear into action because of our love.

Right now, our children are being threatened—but it is insidious and hard to see because the threat comes from how we live in an industrialized and digital world. We know intuitively that this lifestyle feels uncomfortable, but many of us have resigned ourselves to assuming this is the way it has to be for us to have safety and security. This is an illusion and a dangerous one at that.

We can see the harm being done if we only look around us. A few years ago, my area in Southern California was rocked with four teen suicides in a span of three weeks; the youngest was 13. One death, in particular, had a lasting impact because 16-year-old Patrick Turner left behind three suicide notes detailing the reasons for his suicide.[1] He addressed one to his public high school, one to his family, and one to his community. Patrick described the unrelenting expectations he felt to fit into our cultural mold:

So much pressure is put on kids to do good, and a lot of kids make mistakes. One slip-up makes a kid feel like the smallest person in the world. You are looked at as a loser if you don't go to college or if you get a certain GPA or test score. . . . So much pressure is placed on the students to do well that I couldn't do it anymore. There is never a moment to brake.

Although he was a star athlete and a good student who showed no sign of anxiety or depression, his despair was evident in his notes. Despair is suffering without meaning.

Responding to Patrick's suicide, Principal Sean Boulton of a neighboring high school wrote in a letter to the school community saying:

Our teachers and District have simply created and maintained a system that our community/country has demanded from us over the past 20 years since college admissions mania went into hyperdrive, since vocational training programs were dismantled, and since earning "A's" in AP classes became the norm.

Our teachers feel the pressure, administration and counseling feel the pressure, and now parents/students are really feeling the pressures. When we grew up nobody asked us what our GPA was, and it was "cool" to work on the roof of a house. This competitive culture has significantly impacted our young adults. We endlessly discuss test scores, National Merit Scholarships, reading scores, AP scholars, comparisons to other school Districts and this is when we start losing our collective souls—and our children.

He went on to say:

We often shield our students from failure. We think that earning a "C" grade in a class is the end of the world, and we don't allow our students to advocate for themselves. We have also devalued a military career, a plumbing or welding job, and we are a little embarrassed if our children wish to attend vocational training schools instead of a major university.

Lastly, Principal Boulton talked about the diversity of interests and the value of effort:

We say hooray for those students who enter the armed forces, who want to work with their hands, who don't want to be weighed down with the burden of being perfect in high school, and who earn a "C" in a tough class and are proud of themselves. ALL of us as a community have to get to this point if we want to avoid our students feeling shamed, isolated, or worthless.

A FRAGILE LOVE

All our mass production models, whether related to humans, plants, or farm animals, have led us to a vicious cycle of destruction. In every case where we have tried centralized, large-scale command and control methods, we have created toxic environments. Ignoring the diverse and vital ecosystems necessary for health and protection runs contrary to the laws of nature.

We have created "monocrops" that isolate species from their ecosystems of support and mine them for specific outputs. In the case of children, we batch them by age and mine them for certain types of intelligence. In all industrial environments, we have to chemically infuse living organisms to squelch the distress. We use synthetic chemical fertilizers for plants, antibiotics for farm animals, and a multitude of pharmaceutical drugs for humans. Because all these systems interrelate, they have resulted in widespread unhealthy conditions for all.

As James Baldwin said, "*Loving anybody and being loved by anybody is a tremendous danger, a tremendous responsibility.*" We cannot escape the continual changes happening in life, nor the fact that guilt, suffering, and death are an inextricable part of being human. Our desire to avoid these and express our love through fear-based protectiveness has led to fragility and institutional dependence.

In his book *Antifragile: Things That Gain from Disorder*, risk analyst Nassim Nicholas Taleb describes a continuum with fragile at one end, resilience in the middle, and antifragile at the other end.[2] *Fragile* is something easily breakable and unable to withstand adverse conditions, like a teacup. *Resilience* is the ability to stay unchanged when something happens, to bounce back. *Antifragile* is the ability to grow from change and adversity, like how our bodies build muscle and adapt to viruses.

We have reinforced our children's fragility by confining them to industrial-age systems inside buildings where mistakes are discouraged;

where exposure to experiences, multiage relationships, and exploration is limited; and where a culture of sameness suppresses their individuality. They are ill-prepared to weather the storms of life and often fear the future. Many emerge from their years of schooling completely lost, with feelings of meaninglessness and little-to-no understanding of who they are or what they want to become.

According to Stanford professor Jo Boaler, "*The brain sparks and grows when we make a mistake, even if we are not aware of it, because it is a time of struggle; the brain is challenged and the challenge results in growth.*"[3] Struggle and challenge also create resilience and antifragility. **By trying to ensure success without failure, we deprive our children of important developmental steps needed for strong, independent adulthood.**

Antifragility is what I want for my children; the ability to face life head-on, deal with uncertainty, and grow from adversity. But they, like so many in their generation, believed our promise of future success and happiness if they just followed the prescribed path of academic attainment. As recent life events have unfolded, including a worldwide pandemic that created widespread personal and economic upheaval, they have become frustrated by the reality they are forced to contend with. The rallying cry of their generation is, "*This is* not *how it is supposed to be!*"

I have a living, breathing counterpoint to the "supposed to be" narrative: my 94-year-old mother. She was born in 1929, raised during the Depression, and came of age during World War II. There was so much uncertainty and upheaval that she learned to look only at "what is" and figure out how to respond. Her antifragility shined when my father died in 2019 and she had to quarantine alone in the home they had shared, and when she decided to move into a senior care facility so she could socialize more.

My mother knows that life is, always has been, and always will be uncertain. Personal pandemics happen throughout life. She transforms her fears into love, doing what she can in any given moment and sharing herself with others. My daughters have a great role model in their grandmother. My hope for them is that when they encounter unexpected challenges in life—as they most certainly will—they do not sit and scream, "*This is* not *how it is supposed to be!*" I hope, instead, that they put their hands on their hips, look at the situation as it is, and say, "*Now, what can I do about this?*"

SOCIETAL FRAGILITY

Overcoming our societal fragility involves a shift in focus—moving from an attitude of "*what's in it for me*" to "*what am I meant to contribute to this situation.*" The constant comparison to others enforced in our education systems has kept our children's attention on their performance and themselves. It is difficult for them to see their uniqueness as an important contribution, but communities are similar to symphonies. Every instrument—and every note from each instrument—adds to the collective to make a beautiful sound. Every individual is needed.

We must help our children understand that every person has the responsibility to make the most of the life they have been given. We can tell them that they are like a malleable puzzle piece—to be specially formed and forged by them throughout their lives—that will ultimately fit into an unknowable, universal puzzle. Their decisions at every moment, guided by their intuitive conscience, will help them create the shape of their puzzle piece. Parents, communities, and societal expectations can negatively affect outcomes when our well-meaning attempts influence the puzzle pieces that are theirs alone to shape.

Trusting in the necessity of our unique contribution plays a powerful role in overcoming fear. When we engage in meaningful pursuits, we tend not to spend much time on fear. We may know it is lurking, but we stay focused on listening to our inner guidance and doing what we can. We see examples of this in well-known figures such as Nelson Mandela, Rosa Parks, Mother Teresa, Gandhi, and Martin Luther King Jr., but there are millions of others who knowingly or unknowingly understand this as well.

If we love our children, why do we teach them to suppress their inner guidance and devalue their individuality? Why is their worthiness tied to complying and conforming to standardized systems? We lament their lack of self-regulation and independent thinking as they grow, but it should not come as a surprise. It is what we have taught them.

As they progress through different graduation markers of achievement, they must line up rank and file and move across a stage as their name is mentioned for a fleeting moment. We proudly sit and cheer at their "achievement." But do we really see them? Do we know what meeting our expectations costs them mentally, physically, and emotionally?

We tell them that all their sacrifices are for their own good. Are they? At the same time, we tell ourselves that this adherence to our cultural validation norms is an expression of our love for them. The denying of their unique being is not love; it is an expression of fear. Fear that they won't learn what we think they need to know. Fear that they won't fit into our society. Fear that they won't be able to find work. But the reality is that this fear-based approach is not producing the results we desire for most of our children. Rather, it is limiting their potential contributions that we may not even be able to envision.

No matter how well-meaning our efforts to help our children may be, they are misguided. Alex often says, "*Well-meaning is the opposite of meaning.*" *Well-meaning* imposes external perspectives, understanding, and values on our children. *Meaning* is specific to them and something they discover on their own. As with learning, they are born with an orientation toward meaning. It is as natural as breathing oxygen, and they only notice it when it's missing.

FEAR OF THE UNKNOWN

Teaching children the same content in the same way decade after decade does not prepare them for the unknown tomorrows they will face. Trying to forecast the unknowable future based on past knowledge has been futile. It has resulted in their diminished ability to cope with life's inevitable trials and reinforced fear of the unknown. Sadly, our attempts to generate certainty in an uncertain world have created a culture of sameness and a discontented society.

We have suppressed human potential by not honoring our children's individuality, promoting their decision-making abilities, and encouraging their responsibility to contribute their uniqueness to the world. We have frayed our social fabric by not giving the carpenter and the artist the same level of dignity as the scientist and engineer. In reality, our systems were designed for inequality, and their framework continues to generate societal inequities.

In his book *The School and Society*, psychologist and education reformer John Dewey advocated for young people to have responsible independence in how they thought in order to create a free and democratic social system.[4] Independent thinking does not happen in contrived settings geared toward specific answers; it happens in communities addressing real challenges.

Communities offer opportunities to explore curiosities and develop multigenerational relationships. These open ecosystems are available to us if we choose to break down the confining walls of school and encourage our children to interact with a broader world. This can happen after school, on weekends, or by choosing an alternative method of schooling. We need only create the space for meaningful pursuits by deciding where to spend our time and energy. When grades and test scores aren't prioritized, opportunities for exploration and engagement open up.

Learning is innate, relational, and contextual. When we are

interested in something, we learn about it on our own or with and through others. Have you ever seen a child with a passion for dinosaurs? They will want to know everything they can about dinosaurs. They will search books, visit museums, and play with toy models to learn. Education happens everywhere and in a variety of ways. Human beings are creators, and life is a continual creation process.

The ancient Chinese philosopher Confucius described the necessity of experiences in his quote: "*I hear and I forget, I see and I remember, I do and I understand.*" Our children don't need more instruction, they need experience to gain the confidence needed to navigate through life with meaning and purpose. As they become more confident in their decision-making abilities through trial and error, we become more confident in them. There is no greater joy than watching your child conquer self-doubt and move steadfastly in the direction of their dreams.

OVERCOMING OUR FEARS

Facing our fears is one thing; overcoming them is another. We often spend time worrying about possible dangers to our children when they are away from us and not confined to a space we perceive as safe, like school. TV, movies, constant news broadcasting, and up-to-the-minute social media posts keep threats alive in our environments. A kidnapping in Ohio will be broadcast in our living rooms or pop up on our cellphones. Upcoming news and headlines promote negative possibilities to hook audiences, thus reinforcing our society of fear. (Real threats, like living in a crime-ridden area, are different from the imagined threats I am talking about.)

In his book, *Protecting the Gift: Keeping Children and Teenagers Safe (and Parents Sane)*, Gavin de Becker shares insight from his extensive experience providing security for high-net-worth families.[5] His advice on addressing fear boils down to a single innate resource we all have but often ignore: our intuition. Our intuitive sense, like all our other senses, informs us about the world around us and is always for our benefit. It signals us about the presence of danger and is activated in response to something we perceive (a reality).

According to de Becker, unwarranted fear or worry relates to our imagination or memory, not something we perceive in our environment. Trusting our intuition, our "gut feeling," about something or someone is not only valuable for us as we seek to protect our children but essential to teach our children as well. This critical life lesson is an expression of our love and desire to keep them safe.

Love involves trust. We need to trust ourselves and them. More importantly, our children need to learn self-trust so they can discern who to trust as they engage with the world. This ability only comes from experience—at first with us coaching them, then with them on their own. This is a critical step and a responsibility we have before sending our children into the world. Parenting from the passenger seat is about teaching our children to take the wheel and engage with the road themselves so they gain confidence in their abilities.

As a parent, I know this is a hard one. Our desire to protect our children is strong, and protecting them before they can protect themselves is essential. I remember when my first daughter was born, I couldn't believe they let me take her home from the hospital without a detailed "how to" manual. I wanted to do everything right. I bought books about parenting and read them cover to cover. One, in particular, was about positive parenting. I didn't want to say the negative word "no," so I would say "not for Emily" when she reached for an electrical outlet, or anything related. If I could have bubble-wrapped her without worrying about suffocation, I would have figured out how to do that too.

But I quickly came to my senses and realized that I was trying to do something in contradiction to the fundamental laws of human nature. Life is like a giant ledger with pluses and minuses, positives and negatives. Both sides must have entries that balance each other out. Struggles and pain on one side result in resilience and strength on the other. By focusing on only one side of the balance sheet, we deny our children the ability to grow into healthy adulthood with a solid sense of self.

I had to discipline myself to let the worrying thoughts flow through my head and go back out. The reality was that I couldn't always be there to protect my children, especially during their adolescent years. They needed to know that I trusted them to handle the situations they found themselves in and be responsible for the choices they made. I told them I would always walk with them through any consequences of bad choices, but the consequences were theirs to face.

I did not electronically track my children—but always kept my phone near me when they were out of the house. This was my compromise, and I had come a long way. My youngest daughter was born in 2001, the year my oldest daughter started preschool. It was also the year when 9/11 brought us face-to-face with ever-present terrorism. I was part of the parenting generation that was fed twenty-four-hour news feeds about all the terrible things happening in the world. The freedoms I had growing up, like wandering the neighborhood and walking to school, were not available to my children. In fact, laws were passed in many places to punish parents who gave their children these freedoms.[6]

Technology has afforded us the ability to track our children's every move. Although this can provide us with relief and a sense of control, it doesn't mean it is the best thing for our children. Unfortunately, it can send a message that they can't be trusted and that they are responsible for alleviating our fears and anxieties. It keeps the responsibility for their safety on us, not them. It tells them the world is a bad place and that other people can't be trusted if they need help. When our children are away from us, we cannot always get to them quickly. If we don't trust them, how do they learn to trust themselves? They need to trust themselves to handle the situations they find themselves in and find people nearby if they need help.

By allowing them to learn on their own, we are inviting mistakes, struggles, and pain. In her brilliant TED Talk "The Gift and Power of Emotional Courage," psychologist Susan David says:

> *Only dead people never get stressed, never get broken hearts, never experience the disappointment that comes with failure. Tough emotions are part of our contract with life. You don't get to have a meaningful career or raise a family or leave the world a better place without stress and discomfort. **Discomfort is the price of admission to a meaningful life.***

Seeing our child's discomfort is hard for any parent. Our modern era has created ways that give us the feeling of command over their struggles and safety. But this comes at a price. It has limited their explorations and experiences. During the forty-year gap between my childhood and my children's, it was eerie to see the rapid change in childhood freedom. Most notable was the significant decline in unstructured play. The loss of multi-age play and multigenerational connections have left a void in essential human learning—the type of learning that prepares our children for life.

MONSTER LESSONS

My favorite parenting book is *Frankenstein* by Mary Shelley. This often comes as a surprise to people, but the story is extremely relevant to being a parent. It is about creation, responsibility, and our basic need to be loved. As parents and custodians of children, we have a responsibility for how we raise them, for their care and well-being, and for how we release them into the world.

In the book, Dr. Frankenstein set out with high hopes of creating the perfect being, but the creature he brought to life was not what he expected. Overwhelmed, he ran away and left the creature to fend for himself in the world. He turned over responsibility to a terrorized community rather than caring for his creation. There is a heartbreaking moment in the book when the creature describes his desire to be loved. He asks Dr. Frankenstein to create a companion like himself whom he could love. His request is refused, and the doctor runs away again. The immense pain the unloved creature felt is then discharged on the people Dr. Frankenstein cares about most. Ultimately, they both end up devastated and alone with a trail of destruction behind them—all because of the need for love and acceptance.

What is our responsibility toward loving our children? How do we express it? Too often, they become conduits of our unrealized hopes and dreams, our perspectives about how the world works, and our desires for their (and our) status in society. We get frustrated when they don't adhere to our image of who they should be and don't perform in the way we want. We view financial success as the pinnacle of a good life and the education system as the guaranteed ticket. **In truth, the greatest gift we can give them is to authentically love them for who they are—as they are right now.**

Love signifies dignity, respect, and value. All close relationships require that we feel seen, cared for, and special to the people who are important to us. This is especially true for children, as their young lives are shaped by the unconscious interactions of daily life.

Parenting *is* love. While they are young, we are the guardians of the unique beings we brought into the world or have been blessed to care for, and we have a responsibility to honor their continual process of becoming. It doesn't matter if there is a genetic connection. The power of parenting is based on the shared love, the muddling through, and the anchoring against the inevitable storms of life.

But parenting requires more than one-on-one interaction with our children, and we cannot do this on our own. For most of human history, children were raised in communal ecosystems of support—tribes, clans, villages, extended families, and neighborhoods. As the modern world moved faster and grew more complex, we became less confident in our abilities to prepare our children for their future and increasingly relied on institutional systems for support.

At the same time we were shifting responsibility to these systems, we reduced our communal networks to an isolated nuclear family. Our village circles and town squares largely disappeared in favor of organized social silos of work and school, supplemented by organizations related to church, sports, and other activities. The pressure on parents to be all things for their children has become relentless. With many families headed by a single parent, sometimes working multiple jobs, this level of responsibility is overwhelming and often debilitating.

Even with all the resources available to me, my decision to be the primary caregiver for my children was sometimes lonely and exhausting. My deep desire for connection led me to actively cultivate community as best I could. I prioritized the time we spent with grandparents, extended family, neighbors, and friends. We celebrated birthdays and religious rituals and marked rites of passage like graduations. I hosted class and team gatherings to get to know parents and children in our community. I found support from these activities, like carpools and playdates, but most of all, I found friendships. Still, when my children changed grade levels, activities, or schools, I needed to seek new ways to engage with others in my community. Situationally based social interactions usually only last a relatively short time.

Communal ecosystems of support are desperately needed. **Institutional systems cannot take care of people; people have to take care of people.** There are too many unwritten rules of human interaction required for nurturance, and it is beyond the job description of the institution. Like the organized barn raisings of yesteryear, we can support each other in building the kind of environments that promote human flourishing. We can consider all the children in a community as our own, for the health and well-being of each of them affect the health and well-being of all of us.

FACING THE REALITIES OF LIFE

As I learned from my mother, navigating life—with all its uncertainty—begins with the acceptance of "what is" in any given moment and in any given situation. Once we have acceptance, we can listen to our inner guidance about what we can specifically do to respond. No one else can do exactly what we can because no one is exactly the same as us. While we are individuals, we are also part of communities. The dance between our responsibility to ourselves and the communities to which we belong is ongoing. Too much focus on individuality hinders community; too much focus on community hinders individuality. A delicate balance must be sought.

Transforming our fear into action requires orienting ourselves outward. Rather than being concerned only for ourselves and our own children, we can broaden our responsibilities to loving others and caring for the children of our friends and neighbors. We can help with a meal, offer to watch the children at a local park, or become a mentor around a shared interest. We can also care for our planet and the other species we share the ecosystem with; our lives literally depend on it. We are stewards and custodians of each other and everything in our interconnected web of life.

Feeling fear about our children's well-being is a normal part of parenting. Fear and love can both be present, but we must choose which one to focus on. When we change ourselves, we change the world. It is as simple as that. There is a ripple effect, and all our contributions joined together become a wave of change. Our courage can be shown in the daily decisions we make to honor our intuitive knowing.

Many forms of love nourish human beings, but perhaps the most important love of all is the love of self. The gift of life and the responsibility to do what we can with our time is so precious that every moment is valuable. It is with this understanding and trust in our intuitive compass that we show up with aliveness, and this aliveness can energize the world.

It is only in the present moment that love is truly expressed and meaning is pursued. These are interactive experiences in response to people and situations we encounter in the here and now. When we keep the focus on the future, as we do in our modern life, it generates anxiety because there are too many unknowable variables and no real interactions. The anxiety created by these imagined circumstances can translate to fear, and fear generates a flight, fight, or freeze response in us. But love is a greater force than fear.

The ecosystem we are a part of is constantly evolving and changing through our individual and collective actions—so why not intentionally change it for the better? We can spend our time and energy railing against the industrial and digital systems, or we can spend our time and energy being responsible for contributing to the world we believe is possible. There is no turning over the responsibility; we ourselves must be involved.

What's love got to do with it? Everything. It has the power to transform the energy created by fear into responsible action.

———

PART II

WHAT WE CAN DO

CHAPTER 4

WHAT'S A PARENT TO DO?

The journey of a thousand miles begins with a single step.

—Lao Tzu

My evolution as a parent, which is still a work in progress and always will be, has been shaped by my love for my daughters, my deep desire to be connected to them, and my responsibility as their role model. Even though they were each born from the same gene pool and raised in the same environment, their individual human spirits make each of them different. Their uniqueness shapes our family, and our family shapes them. Our community and societal norms also play influential roles.

Emily, Rachel, and Allison remain my greatest teachers. My responsibility to model for them, which at times has felt like a burden, has been a gift. It has broken me open to embrace the process of becoming, to challenge the concept of the perfect parent (impossible), and to develop the courage to share my authentic self so they will be inspired to do the same.

By the time I became the mother of three, I was in my early forties. I had experienced a lot of life, had a career, and could financially support myself. I married a successful entrepreneur whose business was bought by venture capitalists when our children were young. We had the availability of resources not accessible to most people, even though these could not save us from parental guilt, family addictions, incurable illness, or the death of loved ones. My perspective is based on the life I have lived. Not one of us will have the same perspective because not one of us lives the exact same life, even if we are raised in the same home or community. When you have resources, you can give your child advantages in adhering to societal norms. You can ensure they spend their days devoted to tasks given to them by teachers, tutors, and coaches so their grades, test scores, and college résumés are exemplary. But what happens if you don't believe that this is the best thing for them? What happens if you worry that this will devalue their uniqueness, discourage exploration, and limit their potential? What happens if you don't follow the expected protocols like your friends and neighbors?

In this chapter, I share the principles and ideas I learned through my family's experiences as we navigated our way through my children's formative years. Each family's values and priorities will be different and affect the choices they make. Also, the reality is that many of us depend on institutional systems and can't just suddenly leave them. Our society's social infrastructure is tightly woven into these organizational frameworks. However, we can begin to build a new community-based ecosystem that runs parallel to the current structure while we are still engaged with it. Our choices, attitudes, and actions will generate the bridges necessary to create the change we would like to see.

It is easier to connect the dots in hindsight than it is to make the moment-to-moment decisions necessary to progress through life. Our family muddled through, made mistakes, changed our minds, feared, fought, loved, and co-created the family we treasure today—which includes amicably divorced parents and geographic separation.

WHERE ATTENTION GOES, ENERGY FLOWS

As parents, we are the primary influences in our children's lives, and what we reflect to them about their worthiness will help buffer them from some of the serious societal challenges we are facing, especially the massive institutional failures. From our seat beside them, we can support their meaningful pursuits and encourage them to expand their relationships to gain the confidence necessary to face whatever life brings. They need to be ready for life with the coping skills required to weather the storms.

The only constant in life is change. The future is ever-evolving based on the decisions and contributions we make in the present. As John Dewey noted, each person needs a different kind of support in order to flourish.[1] We must create environments that promote human flourishing.

We've tried the standardized, one-size-fits-all approach to living, and we've also tried bubble-wrapping our children for protection against life's inevitable struggles. These clearly didn't work. In fact, they have hindered the ability of many of our children to learn to navigate life on their own. There is no set of instructions or "how to" guides for life because each of us has different characteristics, circumstances, and situations that need to be considered. It is ridiculous to think we can shape a unique human into a common mold and have a positive outcome. Our differences are desperately needed to create the essential diversity required for the health and well-being of everyone in our community.

The following principles are meant to support families who want to shift some of the responsibilities for raising their children back to themselves and their communities. They apply regardless of the type of school (public, private, homeschool, etc.) a child attends or the number of resources a family has available to them. They apply only to what we have control over in our own homes. Each of us can be a ripple—small or large—that spreads change throughout our communities. These principles are some of the ways we can honor and express our love to our children.

Model values and responsibilities

Perhaps the greatest moment of relief for me as a parent came when I realized that I couldn't control my children's choices and behaviors by telling them what they should do; I could only control myself and what I modeled to them. Through experiences in my life with loved ones struggling with addiction, I realized that I really couldn't save the people I cared about by wanting something for them that they didn't want for themselves. I didn't have that power or responsibility. *Responsibility* is "the ability to respond," which belongs to the person in the situation.

When my daughter Emily entered high school and challenged me about how she spent her time, I remembered my important life lessons. I didn't want to police her. I didn't want to be her manager. I wanted to be her mother, her admirer, and her champion. Although I didn't always meet these goals, I did my best to keep them as my North Star.

This shift in focus from them to me was freeing. I could inspire and guide, but my only real control was over my own choices and behaviors. This is much easier than spending time and energy trying to coerce children into submission—although I tried that route too. Carrots and sticks might work in the short term, but they don't work in the long term. Trying to make children care about subjects they don't care about or devote time and energy to meaningless tasks at home and school does little to truly educate them. The root of the word *educate* is "educe"—to draw out, not put in.

Truth be told, we cannot force any human being (or plant or animal, for that matter) to do or be what we want without consequences for them or us. This is an important lesson in all types of relationships. Our well-meaning interventions can result in internal distress or rebellion rather than change. **Why have we allowed our children's worthiness in our society to be defined by a letter, number, or piece of paper?** Why are we so focused on trying to fix our children's behaviors when they don't fit into the rigid system? How is this working for us?

I often wonder whether all of the new pathologies being diagnosed by psychologists and labels being applied to children are adaptive behaviors to the tightly controlled, competitive environments they are raised in. It relieves parents and children when a diagnosis or label is applied (ADHD, OCD, Oppositional Defiant Disorder, and so on). Many exclaim, "*We now know what is wrong with them and can fix it!*" This often means some form of medication. Our urgent desire to fix "the problem" (i.e., the child) can create additional challenges, such as significant side effects from medications as well as potential long-term effects on the child's developing brain and ability to develop coping mechanisms. All the while, we ignore the context of their lives. **We need to fix our society, not our children.**

Because each home situation is different and each child's personality is unique, there is no perfect template for parenting or perfect parents. The best thing we can do is to model the qualities we value as best we can and prioritize their importance in our homes. As Rumi said, "*Yesterday I was clever, so I wanted to change the world. Today I am wise, so I am changing myself.*"

This power to change ourselves is with us regardless of our circumstances. In 2009, I met an extraordinary woman whose story of personal responsibility showed how this can change the course of future generations. Her name is Trinity Wallace-Ellis,[2] and she is now a dear friend and one of the most inspiring women I know. I got to know Trinity when she came to speak at a camp that reunited siblings separated in the foster care system (which most siblings are) called Camp to Belong. I was a volunteer, and her story floored me.

Trinity was born to a pimp and drug dealer father and a sex worker and addict mother. When she was 9 years old, her mother's boyfriend murdered her 2-year-old sister, and her mother left to be with him.

She gave Trinity some money and food to take care of her five younger sisters, but this didn't last long. Soon they were separated into different foster homes where they experienced further physical, sexual, and emotional trauma. Trinity felt a strong sense of responsibility to show her sisters the way and wanted to make different choices than her parents and grandparents. She managed to graduate high school after attending seventeen different schools.

Trinity had a baby at 16. Within a few months, she met a wonderful man, Taj, whom she married. Together, they had a son. Their strong bond supported each other and their families throughout their lives together. Trinity became a strong advocate for foster youth, developing programs to support them and speaking on their behalf. I have had the pleasure of being involved in many of her programs over the years. Despite repeated tragic events in her life, especially the recent unexpected death of her beloved husband, she continues the hard, meaningful work of being a role model for her children, her family members, and the foster youth she works with. Her focus on changing herself, regardless of her circumstances, allowed her to break the generational cycle of foster care for her children and, now, her grandchildren.

With society in disarray, we have come to focus on preparing our children to be changemakers—an oxymoron in standardized systems because innovative change requires the agility and creativity discouraged in these environments. Rather than waiting for our children to become the changemakers of tomorrow, we adults must model what it means to be a changemaker today. We can show our children the way. We can engage in our own meaningful pursuits, responsibly contribute, and prioritize present-moment engagement over future outcomes.

Being present is how we truly see and acknowledge each other. It is the highest form of love. This is hard to do in a fast-paced world that often leaves us exhausted. Being present is a constant struggle for me, as it is for most parents. It requires conscious effort, which is best achieved when we are rested—which is also difficult when parenting. However, if we do not replenish ourselves, we are unable to fully be present with others. We cannot do this alone; we need to rely on others for help. This is why local communities are so important.

There are many things that I wish I had done differently as a parent, but one in particular stands out: I wish I took fewer photos. I wish I did not have a lens separating me from my children at the many experiences and events we shared. I spent a lot of time trying to document their lives instead of living the moment with them. I think back to when they were on a school stage, and they saw my camera instead of my face smiling at them. While our family photos and videos are treasured by all of us, there are too many of them, and the idea of organizing them "someday" overwhelms me. Now, with cameras on phones, I see my children living their lives behind the lens. Part of this is attributable to our cultural norms, but it is also because I modeled it to them.

We are not machines; we are human beings in the never-ending process of becoming and learning as we go. This muddling through is another important thing we can model for our children. For many years, I put pressure on myself to try and do everything right. It is not humanly possible and was not beneficial for any of us—plus, it was exhausting. Was I modeling for them that I never made mistakes? We can't be machine-like in our productivity, efficiency, or timing of results. When we have self-compassion for our own human failings on the road to becoming, we can have compassion for others. This is one of the most loving things we can do as we all attempt to answer the demands of life and address our serious challenges. It is how we will shift paradigms.

Prioritize values

Trade-offs must be made to create time and space for exploration and relational engagement in the real world. Our family set some priorities that expressed our values and used them as a measure against which we could evaluate desired activities. Remembering that the present moment is all we have, and recognizing that the future is unknown *and* unknowable, can go a long way in determining how best to prioritize time.

We defined three priorities in the early years: 1) relationships, especially multigenerational and peer-related; 2) dinnertime; and 3) experiences outside of school. All three of these were prioritized over externally mandated tasks. They needed to be adjusted slightly as our family evolved, but they were helpful when we were making decisions about activities and commitments.

Dinnertime had to be moved around as my daughters grew and became more independent, but it remained a strong priority. Our compromise was to decide which nights we would all agree to have dinner together (or switch the type of meal we shared when dinners weren't feasible). The dinner table is an important way for children to learn to share their views and respectfully listen to others' views. The "respectfully listen" part was hard to adhere to, and many meals were spent with everyone talking over each other. As my daughters grew, though, it became easier to hold discussions where everyone had an opportunity to voice their opinion.

No subject was off-limits at our table, and the conversations became more intense as my daughters entered their teen years and were exposed to different ideas. We talked about controversial issues of the day such as abortion, gay marriage, and white privilege. After listening to them share their perspectives, I reevaluated some of my views. Luckily, cell phones weren't a thing I had to contend with until high school, and they were banned from our dinner table from the start.

Why should families, especially single-parent households, have to devote their limited time together to schoolwork *at home* rather than truly engaging with one another? The dinner table offers a valuable model for democratic dialogue and learning to listen to others' viewpoints.

I always built in time for our family to bond, so it was established as an important part of our schedule. But sometimes the things I planned ended up being "forced family fun"—missing the fun part for all involved. We also tried family meetings, and I still have the visual of my daughters on the couch with their feet over the back, staring at us from their upside-down positions. As they grew, I understood the importance of including them in the decision-making process of how and when we would spend time together.

I sought their opinions about how we wanted to spend weekends, breaks, and summers, as well as how we could carve out time for each other. It inevitably required compromises. Sometimes we committed to going together to one of their activities or visiting grandparents. The types of vacations we took evolved from visiting museums and learning history (which their father and I enjoyed and thought would be beneficial) to experiences that allowed for a lot of downtime and hanging out. We made sure to value their time with friends and worked that in around family obligations. For example, we would have the grandparents over for an early dinner, and my daughters would go out with friends afterward. This proved to be much more beneficial for all involved, and our commitment to spend time together is still strong today.

The priorities set will vary significantly for each family, depending on interests and circumstances, but setting benchmarks offers a great start. Our family's choices definitely moved us against the achievement culture. We attended family birthdays during the week, even if they competed with tests or assignments. We didn't choose club sports since most would conflict with our dinner hour and consume our weekends. We planned trips months ahead of time and blocked off the calendar.

There is always tension between an individual's needs and their responsibility to be part of a family or community. I remember having to stop at the store on my way home from picking my daughters up from school. They protested because they wanted to go home. I told them, "*I don't always like driving you around to birthday parties and activities either. When we are part of a family, we need to sometimes do things that support each other whether or not we want to do it.*" If we focus too much on accommodating our children's schedules, they believe that they are the center of the world and do not have to compromise for others.

There weren't many other families in our community who shared our priorities, but few challenged our choices. The biggest hurdle I faced was my own children's desire to do what their peers were doing. This is understandable because humans evolved from tribes and being isolated can feel threatening. I had internal battles with myself about how "alternative" to go without detaching them too much from the reality that, in our society, children's social lives are related to school and organized activities. There was no town square where they could gather and hang out. Other kids were in the silo and that is where my children often wanted to be. It was a very frustrating dance.

Some of the trade-offs we made led to disappointment and involved hard choices we all had to make. For example, Rachel was recruited by a Hollywood manager when she was 15 years old. If we signed the contract, her father or I would have to drive an hour and a half (on a good traffic day) back and forth to Los Angeles whenever she had an audition or job. She loved the idea of being able to act professionally and really pushed for us to agree. We discussed how this would affect our family dynamics and her ability to fully commit to her high school community and its arts program, where she could perform with friends. In the end, we decided the disruption was too great and declined to sign the contract. She was at first mad and disappointed, but she went on to enjoy the local arts programs she participated in. After she graduated, she signed the contract herself.

Allison sometimes reminds me of how she wished she could have continued to do gymnastics when she was 5 or 6, but I made her quit. She had so many things she was interested in trying that I told her to choose one at a time. I would have spent all my time driving her and her sisters around to different activities. She decided to switch to karate. While we all still look back at the photo of her perfect hand-stand with a smile, my now 5'10" daughter probably made the best decision.

Sometimes we agreed to compromise so they could participate in a school-related or extracurricular activity with friends, and usually, these were seasonal. As they grew older, they each developed specific interests and wanted time to pursue them. I also insisted that they work hourly jobs or volunteer after they got their driver's licenses, further adding to the busyness of our life. There was a constant search for a middle ground, and with three girls close in age, our calendar was often chaotic despite our best efforts. When it felt like the treadmill was moving faster than we could run, we tried to readjust what we were doing. Through it all, we navigated our way together.

Looking back, the often-messy trade-offs we made were so worth it. Our family will always cherish the memories we shared, especially with grandparents who are no longer here, and the travel adventures we experienced together. We learned many life lessons—sometimes painful, sometimes joyful—while living under the same roof. It is a time we will never get back.

Emphasize character, not grades

While we can't control the emphasis on grades and test scores in schools or our communities, we can control it at home by focusing on charac-ter accomplishments instead. We can show our children that we love *them*, and that the worthiness of our love is not based on performance. Although each of us will approach this differently, I chose not to access the school's online services or monitor when my daughters had tests or assignments due. I felt this was their responsibility. We spent a lot of time at dinner, in the car, and sitting on their beds, talking about their relationships and the activities they were engaged in. With three girls, that mostly meant discussing how they were handling the drama that inevitably arose. We also volunteered together, and this offered a great opportunity to discuss the value of sharing themselves with others.

Character is a much better life success indicator than academic achievement. A child's character is shaped through struggle as they learn how to handle life's ups and downs and how to treat others in the process. If they don't have experiences outside the confines of school buildings or organized activities, it is difficult for them to understand the complexity of life and how to navigate through it.

It was so painful to watch my children struggle with friendships, not perform well in a sport, or not achieve the academic benchmarks they thought "everyone else" could. I remember one of my daughters calling me from school, crying after she had done poorly on a test. She felt so stupid compared to her classmates. My heart hurt for her, and I told her that the score had nothing to do with her smartness or worthiness. I offered to let her change schools since the high school she attended was intense in its approach to academic perfection. (They even had kids who had achieved "honor roll" stand up in assemblies, leaving anyone who didn't stand up feeling exposed and ashamed. On principle, I never attended even if one of my daughters was standing up.) But she wanted to stay with her friends. I told her that if she could learn to be who she was amid all the pressure to be the same as everyone else, she would have mastered a very important life skill.

Focusing on external outcomes, such as grade point averages, test scores, and awards, as the measure of a child's worth is shortsighted. Few people in the real world introduce themselves with their statistics and achievements. Instead, people are judged by their integrity, empathy, and kindness. Those who can interact and collaborate to ensure the success of everyone, as well as the project, will be the ones who benefit the most. We can help our children see that they have control over these important traits, whereas they don't usually have control over external outcomes like highly subjective grades.

A parent who smooths the way (known as a helicopter, lawn-mower, or snowplow parent) is likely to raise a child who doesn't have the necessary self-regulation, self-initiative, or adaptability to navigate life well. Hard lessons will come from meeting all the external mea-surements and still not getting into the university of their choice (if higher education is even an option) or from being the most deserving and not getting the award. But if they know they are valued because of who they are, they will be able to handle these difficult moments.

Character, along with qualities such as collaboration, communica-tion, creativity, and relational intelligence, cannot be learned through textbooks, homework, or standardized testing; they all relate to human interconnectedness. They are also highly valued in the workplace. We can teach these qualities through mindful parenting and exposure to a broader world.

Challenge what institutions prioritize

The forty-year gap between when I grew up and when my children did highlighted the dramatic shift we have undergone from community-centered to school-centered lives. The focus on college résumé build-ing fills many children's schedules and creates a relentless pace of life. Although my daughters were able to enjoy some of their childhood because of our alternative school choice, the school only went to eighth grade, and in high school, we were soon faced with challenging schedule decisions.

They each chose to attend the same private high school, and this is when I began to really see the devastation created by the college mania. I did my best to limit AP classes and other demanding course-work that didn't align with their interests or that would limit time for friendships, family relationships, volunteering, or part-time work, but it was not easy.

I continued to advocate for my children within the system as best as I could during this period, but it was like shoveling snow during a storm. When Rachel joined the high school two years after Emily, I noticed significant changes in the pressure for academic achievement.

I requested a meeting with the principal that was eerily reminiscent of the one I had in 2005 with the elementary school principal. He listened to my concerns and asked me what my expectations were for the school. I told him that I hoped for three things: 1) that my children were honored for their individuality; 2) that my family's time was viewed as sacred and respected; and 3) that my children were allowed to find their own way rather than being molded into a predetermined "success" model.

In a follow-up email, I quoted famous business management expert Clayton Christensen, who noted in his book *How Will You Measure Your Life?* that "*People who are driven to excel have this unconscious propensity to underinvest in their families and overinvest in their careers—even though intimate and loving relationships with their families are the most powerful and enduring source of happiness.*"[3] We encourage our children to overinvest in academic work, sports, arts, and so on, while underinvesting in relationships and meaningful endeavors. I wrote, "*We don't get this time back; neither do they. What are we modeling to them about what we would like their home lives to be like in the future? What are we telling them about the importance of relationships?*"

He kindly acknowledged my concerns and challenges, but as with the previous principal, his hands were tied. With a focus on college-prep, academic achievement and testing were the school's priority. No matter how much they talked about caring for the whole child, every student was pushed toward the same measurable outcomes to ensure college admission.

In addition to the demands placed on children by schools, extracurricular activities entered at warp speed, becoming a Pac-Man of time and money. What used to be recreational became competitive, adult-driven, and an increasingly expensive part of building a college résumé. What used to involve two or maybe three days a week became five days a week, plus weekends, and lasted all year round.

Some of this was motivated by the need for scholarships and the illusion that they were readily available to all talented students, some from wanting a child to be good at something, and some from seeking friendships and community. But this type of community, like schools, ends when our children age out. Socially, they are forced to move from one adult-controlled silo to another rather than having a broad, ongoing community of support and unstructured time with peers.

Why are we not questioning the endless, time-sucking tasks required of our children? Why have we allowed their lives to become so structured and routine? Why do we delude ourselves into thinking that if someone tells them something and tests them, they have learned it? Leonardo da Vinci once said, **"*Studying without a liking for it spoils the memory and it retains nothing it takes in.*"**

Free play—initiated and directed by children—is nature's way of teaching them the necessary lessons about life and is critical to their development into independent-thinking adults, according to research professor Peter Gray.[4] Rather than studying how children learn in school—which is akin to studying animal behavior in a zoo—he studies hunter-gatherer tribes to understand evolutionary learning. His research shows that our war on childhood is detrimental to our children's ability to learn to navigate their own way.

Gray's regular *Psychology Today* column provides important per-spectives all parents could benefit from. One of his columns, titled "The Culture of Childhood: We've Almost Destroyed It," discusses the loss of childhood learning through play as we have sought, in vain, to control who and what they can become:

In play amongst themselves, children create their own activities and solve their own problems rather than rely on a powerful authority figure to do these for them. This is one of the great values of playing away from adults. In such play

they have to, as it were, be the adults, precisely because there are no adults present.
Play is the practice space for adulthood. Adults spoil this large purpose of play
when they intervene and try to be helpful.[5]

Compulsory schooling was founded on control and obedience to authoritarian directives. In modern times, this premise has expanded to include the molding and shaping of workers for our consumer-driven economy. Sadly, our children's time has been allocated to adult-determined tasks and activities. As parents, we can make a concerted effort to change that.

Encourage multi-age relationships

In addition to the essential role peers play in the development of children, intergenerational relationships are also very valuable. Whether family or not, these represent powerful forces of love and acceptance that benefit both the younger and older participants. If family relations are geographically or emotionally unavailable, neighbors and community members can be extremely beneficial. Relationships with caring adults are fundamental to well-being. My children were fortunate to have all four of their grandparents nearby when they were growing up, and I made sure they could spend time with them regularly. They shared many treasured moments together.

Aunts, uncles, godparents, and close friends were particularly helpful to me when I felt like I sounded like Charlie Brown's teacher to my children (wah wah wah). I knew my children were surrounded by people who cared about them and would listen to the things they said, mentoring them in their areas of interest and supporting their responsibilities in caring for younger children. All these relationships have contributed to their overall community of support for both personal and professional endeavors.

Real-world interaction lets our children be seen, appreciated, and loved as something other than a numerical statistic. It provides them with a broader context from which to view themselves and the world around them. It also allows them to explore and discard potential pathways before making a substantial investment. Part-time work, volunteering, internships, and job shadowing all provide great learning experiences and the opportunity for self-assessment to determine what they want to do next. Supportive adults riding alongside them play a vital role in all these areas.

Get educated about the reality of college

This is probably one of the most important things we can do for our children, and I stumbled upon it by chance, as I described in the Introduction. Both the nature of college life and the character of our economy have radically transformed in recent decades. Although some colleges (generally small) adhere to their educational mission, most have moved away from this in favor of a business model that uses mass-marketing campaigns to recruit students. **Students have been reduced to consumers of a credentialing product rather than seekers of learning experiences for their unique growth and development.**

The more select the colleges are perceived to be by their high ranking on published lists of "best colleges," the more desirable they are to students and families. It is actually a numbers game because the more students who apply for the fixed number of spots, the lower their acceptance rate becomes and the higher their ranking. Colleges spend millions on marketing to increase the number of applicants. They also make millions of dollars on the applications.

We have come to believe that well-known schools sprinkle pixie dust on all students who attend, and they generate well-connected and financially viable futures. However, in reality, the connections are more likely tied to socio-economic level than the school. My experiences with my daughters' schools have shown me how inadequate they are at connecting students to opportunities, let alone opportunities that pay enough to justify the tuition. Also, it doesn't make sense for someone interested in, let's say, regenerative agriculture to attend a well-known school without that major, and perhaps we should question whether they will learn best by obtaining a degree in the field in the first place.

In *Antifragile*, Nassim Nicholas Taleb challenges whether lecture-driven knowledge leads to prosperity for all, and I find his perspective fascinating. His empirical investigation found no evidence that a country's general level of education raised its overall income. In fact, he notes *"the opposite is true, that wealth leads to a rise of education."*[6] The link between education spending and economic growth simply doesn't exist. In other words, it is a societal myth that education leads to wealth for the majority of people. It does, however, create compliant workers.

Earnings are specific to the field of study, and not everyone is interested or able to pursue those fields, yet we prescribe college as a vehicle for everyone to earn the same income level. In some cases, the protocols and time required to meet the necessary requirements can affect stated earnings, even at the highest levels. The long, costly road to obtaining a medical degree is a good example. The length of time required before graduates are full-fledged practitioners can delay the promised earnings until they are close to 30 years old. Add to this an insurance-controlled healthcare system that determines wages, and we can see that pursuing this path may not provide as beneficial a return on investment as it once did.

The entire elementary and secondary education systems are designed to feed the higher education system, not nurture individual human potential. They also feed the textbook, testing, and tutoring industrial complexes. And, sadly, the healthcare system. As mentioned previously, this keeps our children dependent on systems and external validation rather than on becoming independent and authentic decision-makers.

This is not to say that there isn't a need for specific higher education degrees or that some individuals who require them won't reap the benefits. I am challenging the mechanistic, standardized approach that all students must adhere to. Luckily, the winds of change are blowing. Driven by the exorbitant cost of college, the introduction of low-cost credentialing alternatives, and the shift to hiring for skills competency rather than degree attainment, new opportunities are emerging for our children.

As each of my daughters chose to go to college, we established guiding principles to ensure they had skin in the game and would take the investment of time and money seriously. They were required to graduate in four years, and we evaluated their ability to continue yearly. (As discussed previously, most students do not graduate in four years.) Before accepting admission, they had to agree to maintain an annual 3.0 grade point average. Although we did not emphasize grades before college, this parameter helped keep them focused on passing their classes to graduate on time.

I advised my daughters that the first thing they needed to do when they arrived on campus was to find "their people." It was important for them to have a group of friends who could look out for each other and who they could go to for support. Luckily, they were each able to find and nurture reliable friend groups.

Find like-minded parents and support each other
We are designed to be collaborative and belong to communities. We have lost this in relying on institutional systems rather than each other. Hunter-gatherers evolved by sharing the burdens of life and the various tasks that needed to be performed to support themselves and the community. Each person contributed something—cooking, childcare, washing, hunting—often working together. We need to rebuild this in our neighborhoods and communities to combat the isolation created by our modern lifestyle. We need to add a "contribution economy" to the full-time employment economy, the gig economy, and the sharing economy that now make up how we live.

The silver lining to the COVID-19 pandemic was that some

neighbors and communities banded together to support each other. The Nextdoor app was a space where people in need of something, like shopping or a medicine prescription, could find someone to help them. Many people met their neighbors for the first time and began regular interactions. We are not meant to be separate; we are all inter-dependent on each other and our planet.

We need to take care of each other to take care of our children. Parenting is not for the faint of heart; it is a huge responsibility. Dependable support systems are essential to replenishing our strength and fortitude. "*The resilience of children rests on the health and well-being of the primary caregivers,*" says Dr. Suniya Luthar, clinical psychologist, researcher, and founder of AC Groups.[7] She goes on to say that parents can't put their own oxygen mask on first if they are in crisis mode; they need one or two close non-spousal supporters who can put it on for them. The expansion of our communal networks plays an important role in our well-being, and thus, the well-being of our children.

While raising my children, I relied heavily on my best friend from college, Moira Hummel. We never lived in the same city, but I valued her perspective and advice. I was a late bloomer, and Moira had chil-dren a decade before I did. I learned a lot from her. In turn, I provided a sounding board and offered suggestions for her parenting dilemmas. We would visit or call each other regularly to share about our lives and provide support. After nearly forty-five years, we are still putting oxygen masks on each other when needed. When my girls left for college, they expressed the hope of finding their own "Aunt Moira."

It is not always possible to find support within our families of origin, but throughout my life, my sisters, Robin and Cynthia, have acted as sounding boards whenever possible. Robin's husband, Bryan, is also one of my most trusted advisors on business and personal matters. I rely on him to critique my work and challenge my thinking. He is hilarious and loves a good debate, so he makes discussing our differing perspectives fun.

I also joined a neighborhood playgroup when my children were young. We met regularly at local parks, where we exchanged ideas about potty training, activities, schools, and more. While our children played, we engaged in supportive talks, shared laughs, and provided recommendations for resources. These moments proved to be a valuable lifeline of support. Unfortunately, the playgroup disbanded when our children began school, and extracurricular time commitments made regular gatherings difficult.

I strongly encourage finding other parents who are looking to support their children in the same way and figuring out how best to share responsibilities so everyone contributes. I did not want to put my children in preschool before kindergarten, so I found a group of moms who were interested in trading time. Two of us would watch the kids and organize activities while the other had a few hours off to work or take care of other things. We rotated houses a few times a week. Figuring out the sharing of childcare is especially important for single parents who are both breadwinners and primary caregivers. We ought to share these responsibilities for the health and well-being of all our community's children. The vitality and health of our communities is dependent on everyone's contribution.

TIME FOR DISCERNMENT

Sir Ken Robinson, a renowned education advisor to governments, schools, and nonprofits, often noted that we had sacrificed the creative capacities of generations to an academic illusion. When he was asked by policymakers and administrators what to do about the challenges they were facing, like dropout rates, mental illness, and so on, he simply answered, "*Stop causing it.*"[8] The problem lies in the framework of the system we created, not our children.

We are the custodians of our children's potential, especially when they are young. Our love can be a motivating force to overcome our fears. Guilt, like suffering and death, is inextricably woven into human existence. We cannot escape it, and parental guilt is the most distressing. Our children are dependent on us, and this responsibility is huge. Not one of us will get everything right. The term "guilty conscience" is well-seeded in our culture for a reason. Sometimes we unknowingly do something hurtful to our children, and sometimes, we intuitively know when we have done something wrong. Regardless, when we experience guilt, it allows us to decide how to do things differently in the future. We can transform the energy of guilt into corrective action.

There is so much we as parents can do to support our children in learning to navigate their own way, regardless of access to certain kinds of resources. **The non-negotiable starting point begins with honoring and loving the child we have—as they are now.** This means not forcing them to be some societal version of themselves. We have to refrain from making them decide what they want to be while they are in high school without giving them time to explore the real world.

John Glenn was part of the first group of astronauts for NASA. If Glenn had to choose a career in high school, he would never have picked astronaut—it hadn't been invented yet. In his book *How to Find Fulfilling Work*, philosopher Roman Krznaric notes that a lack of experience makes deciding about our future interests difficult when we are a teenager or even a young adult.[9] He describes fulfilling work as something we nurture and grow into; we know it when we are motivated to get up to go do it.

We need to prepare our children for a lifetime of employment disruptions and new possibilities emerging for them. They will be best served by their distinctly human capacities of intuition, adaptability, creativity, critical thinking, compassion, and collaboration. These are learned through childhood play, interest-related experiences, and relationships.

Whenever possible while they are young, we can give our children responsibility for decision-making and encourage the patience and struggle inherent in pursuing meaningful endeavors. As they begin to take the wheel of their own life, we can be alongside them, prompting them to trust themselves and continue on in the face of adversity. We can participate in creating communities of support to encourage long-term relationships and exposure to new opportunities and experiences. In this way, we will build nurturing and loving environments where all our children can reach their full human potential. It might just transform our own lives as well.

———

CHAPTER 5

IS SCHOOL TRANSFORMATION POSSIBLE?

Salvation for our educational ills . . . will have to come from within an educational community willing to say we have met the enemy and it is us.

—Seymour Sarason

I always dreamed of finding a public school for my children that valued their individuality, understood the critical role of relationships, and encouraged broad community interactions. I hoped to find a place where pulling out unique human potential was more valued than pouring in generic content, a place where teachers were trusted guides rather than directors, and where parents could be involved as active partners in their children's academic process rather than being relegated to bake sales. I never found it while raising my children. Then, when researching stories for my blog, I was elated to find this type of school actually existed!

In early 2020, as the world was in a global pandemic lockdown, I watched a webinar called *A New Way Forward*, hosted by Kelly Young of Education Reimagined.[1] One of the panel guests was Carlos Moreno, Co-Executive Director of Big Picture Learning (BPL),[2] an innovative education not-for-profit organization operating a network of over 275 global schools, with approximately 85 in the U.S. (spread across 29 states).

Carlos spoke with deep respect for students as unique individuals and described the value of learning experiences in and out of school. He told a moving personal story about his most important teacher, his grandmother, and described the critical role families and communities can play in a student's academic journey. He clearly understood that learning is relational and contextual, and it was inspiring to hear an educator speak like this.

I wanted to learn more. I came to find out that this innovative model for educating students based on dignity, trust, and respect came about through the efforts of several dedicated individuals. I believe the Big Picture Learning story can be helpful to any parent interested in understanding what is possible in transforming public schools.

The Big Picture Company (the parent entity of Big Picture Learning) began in 1995 when two seasoned educators, Dennis Littky and Elliot Washor, were asked by Rhode Island Superintendent, Peter McWalters, to build a new type of public charter high school from scratch—a school for the twenty-first century that would involve head, heart, hands, and health.

Dennis and Elliot had gained a reputation as transformative education innovators when they were principal and assistant principal, respectively, of the award-winning Thayer High School in New Hampshire, which had been failing before their involvement. They were also concurrently directing professional development around their practice for 500 schools in the U.S. Stanley Goldstein, founder and former CEO of CVS Pharmacy, offered his support to help them foster a similar educational environment in his home state of Rhode Island.

Dennis and Elliot started with the question: "*What's best for kids?*" They wanted students to be at the center of driving their own learning. Their years as teachers, principals, and administrators had shown them that many of the widely accepted theories about learning lacked real-life practicality, ignored the importance of hands-on application, and often disregarded basic human needs. They understood through research about gangs—an ever-present force in the communities they worked in—that young people need to feel a part of a culture, something larger than themselves.

With a common mission to create an environment conducive to meaningful pursuits and strengthen community support for all ages, they built The Met, short for Metropolitan Regional Career and Technical Center. It would become the flagship for all Big Picture schools to follow, as well as other schools in statewide reform initiatives. Big Picture Learning has achieved national and international acclaim for its successful design. In 2010, then-president Barack Obama stated, "*We'll follow the example of places like The Met Center, in Rhode Island, that give students that individual attention, while also preparing them through real-world, hands-on training for the possibility of succeeding in a career.*"

The Met is a living, breathing community ecosystem of learning built in one of the poorest neighborhoods in Providence. Its series of small schools are purposely designed to be open and interactive with the local neighborhood. When I visited, it was the students who showed me around and told their personal stories of learning. (All visitors to The Met are hosted by the students themselves.) Their ease in conversing with adults and their obvious engagement in what they were learning were so impressive. The Met has been changing lives like this for decades; it recently celebrated its twenty-fifth anniversary.

Although I am describing the framework that was ultimately created, both Dennis and Elliot will attest to the bitter struggle they experienced in bringing their vision to reality. There were many defeats and frustrations generated from fighting against large bureaucracies and political players. Out of the many years of practice, mistakes, and lessons learned while designing, building, and operating The Met as well as running national and statewide initiatives based on Big Picture Learning's work, several design distinguishers emerged. Let's take a look.

HUMAN-SCALE, COMMUNITY ENVIRONMENTS

Big Picture schools are built like small villages. They are designed for a human scale where everyone knows each other. The dynamics of smaller schools, with no more than about 130 to 150 students, can foster this type of communal environment, whereas large-scale schools cannot. By virtue of their size, larger schools have to put in place standard operating procedures for communication and efficiency more akin to processing plants than organic ecosystems.

A culture of respect, caring, and trust is created in small environments where each individual can be seen and heard and understands their responsibility to contribute authentically to the community. Dennis says,

> *Culture is the most important thing. If you get the culture right, everything else falls into place. Every action has to be about respect. On the first day of school, we had the kids make the rules for the school. They are always tougher than adults. Our rules are centered on respect—respect for self, others, and the physical space.*

Sometimes Big Picture schools are stand-alone, and sometimes they are schools within schools. They are all public schools, with a small percentage as charter schools; most are built in the most disadvantaged areas of our country—urban, suburban, and rural. Because they respect the neighborhood and the neighborhood respects them, there is a minimal level of graffiti, theft, or vandalism. Safety is enhanced by the culture of respect and caring fostered by students and adults who know each other well. Imagine the nurturing environments we could create for our children if all our monolithic school structures were broken into a series of smaller schools within the larger school and opened to their surrounding communities!

Within Big Picture schools, students are part of a 12 to 16 person advisory lasting for two to four years. The advisor (a teacher) gets to know each student and their family. Big Picture schools strive to have teachers who reflect the students' diverse cultural backgrounds. They all communicate regularly. Advisors help their students create personal Learning Plans and guide them toward discovering Learning through Interests and Internships (LTI) opportunities. They coordinate with community-based mentors and ensure students are prepared for quarterly exhibitions. Advisories are the heart and soul of Big Picture schools. They offer a home base for students and often become a second family.

STUDENTS AT THE CENTER

The Met started with the motto *"One Student at a Time."* The mantra of Big Picture Learning is *"The student is the curriculum; the community is the classroom."* **Each student becomes the driver of their own learning with adults taking turns in the passenger seat.** As Dennis describes it, *"The only really substantial thing education can do is help us to become continuous lifelong learners. . . . Learners who learn without textbooks, tests, certified teachers, and standardized curricula. Learners who love to learn. To me, this is the ultimate goal of education."*

Supported by their advisor, parent or guardian, and sometimes a mentor, students design personalized Learning Plans based on their interests. The definition of what constitutes an interest includes not only hobbies and curiosities but the kinds of problems they see happening in their world that they are interested in solving. Classes on specific subjects, like math and English, enhance their real-world learning and are incorporated into their individualized plan. In addition to Learning Plans, students also prepare post-secondary plans to support their future success, such as college, trades, or the military.

Without the need to follow standardized curricula (there are no

AP classes offered), study for standardized tests, or participate in competitive academic rankings, students have time to explore interests alongside mentors in the community who are actively engaged in their chosen area of interest. Students spend two full days a week dedicated to real-world learning at internships, job shadows, or conducting informational interviews to figure out where they want to start or go next.

The term student-centered (or learner-centered) relates to the individuality of the student—their unique interests, abilities, needs, and circumstances. All these characteristics affect a student's learning. Some educational proponents use the term student-centered, but in reality, the student is at the center of an adult-determined curriculum that has been slightly adjusted for their particular learning style or interest. This is more like programming a robot and not at all similar to how Big Picture Learning defines student-centered.

INTERESTS, RELATIONSHIPS, AND PRACTICE

Elliot says:

> We know that learning happens best when interests, relationships, and practice are woven together. People learn more quickly, more deeply, more comprehensively, and more meaningfully when they are pursuing their interests with skilled people who know them and let them practice, play, make mistakes, start over again, ask questions, test things out and then show what they can do.

The way we organize education into specific classes does not reflect how humans function in the world. Isolating math as a subject (memorizing formulas and doing theoretical exercises) ignores how learning involves making sense of information and connecting it in a real context. **We learn best through hands-on experiences doing things that matter to us, working alongside adults and peers who care about the same thing.** Big Picture schools also start at 9 a.m., when adolescent brains are more fully online.

When students *want* to learn about something and have someone to learn *with,* amazing things happen. *Want* and *with* are important words in the adoption of learner-centered models. Big Picture Learning has found that this approach to learning increases engagement and graduation rates—and more importantly still, their students graduate with a sense of direction, an understanding of how to apply their knowledge, and a community of people to support them as they venture out into the wider world.

DIRECT CONNECTION TO THE COMMUNITY

Real-world learning with mentors who care and share the student's interest is a cornerstone of Big Picture Learning, and it distinguishes them from traditional internships offered through academic institutions. Traditional internships connect adult mentors and students in industries that schools determine would be economically beneficial for the student—regardless of their interests. This is shortsighted as it rarely creates long-term employees. Mentors in these types of internships are often required by the company to take on the intern, but they have little interest or wherewithal to spend the necessary time developing the relationship.

The nurturing of human beings happens in relational communities. *"When the student is ready, the teacher will appear. When the student is truly ready, the teacher will disappear,"* according to the Tao Te Ching. This has been Big Picture Learning's experience. Throughout time, children learned alongside adults in apprenticeships for life and work. The separation of children into mass-production modes of learning has not been successful in preparing our children for life, let alone work.

Another important distinguisher of Big Picture schools is that there is an advisor who monitors the relationship between the mentor and the student. Along with background checks required of all mentors, this provides an extra safety measure. Although these preventative measures are helpful, our children still must learn to intuitively discern safe people and environments. Having a trusted advisor to talk with about concerns is important in helping them learn to validate their intuitive sense.

A few years ago, a technology platform called ImBlaze was built to support the monitoring and connection of students to community mentors. Each school builds its own database facilitated by an LTI coordinator. Students are encouraged to reach out to people they know (grandparents, aunts, friends) to find mentors in their area of interest or even use Google or LinkedIn to identify possibilities. Parents can sign up as mentors and encourage friends to do the same. Lastly, the school's staff (advisors, teachers, and administrators) contribute from their personal networks.

When The Met first opened with fifty students in a disadvantaged area, few thought that they would be able to find mentors for them. They did. In fact, within 6 years, they had a database of 2,000. As of this writing, there are over 43,000 LTI opportunities currently available for students using the ImBlaze platform.

The networking skills learned, and the relationships fostered can provide the basis for finding work throughout their lives. Many companies now encourage employees to recommend people for available positions rather than post the positions because they have found that this type of recruiting outreach fosters a better company culture and generates longer-term employees. The networking effect also applies to the rapidly growing number of independent skilled workers and solopreneurs who work on a project-by-project basis, as this is how they are able to sustain their workflow. **Who you know, who knows you, matters.**

PARENT AND FAMILY INVOLVEMENT

Big Picture Learning's philosophy is that parents are an integral part of their student's education process; therefore, they enroll families as well as students. Parents are active participants in the design of their child's personalized learning plan and attend exhibitions of their children's work every quarter. In addition, parents have numerous opportunities to pursue their own learning and participate in the school community.

Lastly, they play a valuable role in identifying mentors, as well as participating as mentors themselves. I would have loved to be a part of this kind of parent community!

Why are we so convinced that educators know what is best for our children? As Marian Wright Edelman notes, *"Parents forget that they themselves are really the experts."*

With a shared mission to prepare students to live lives of their own design, parents, caring mentors, and the school work together to ensure equitable opportunities are available to each student so they can achieve their greatest potential. Big Picture Learning's website states the following: *"We are friends. We are partners. We are learners and teachers. We are beloved agitators. We are activists."*

Empowered families can shift neighborhood cultures and create environments that promote lifelong learning and human flourishing. Families can build bridges between the school and the community, creating much-needed area revitalization. These contributions provide critical support for change. If we truly want to transform education for our children, we have the responsibility to do our part.

AUTHENTIC ASSESSMENT

Recognizing the uniqueness of each student, Dennis and Elliot understood early on that standardized testing did not adequately reflect a student's true learning. Many aspects of how and what a student learns cannot be measured, and no student can be compared to another. With this in mind, they created quarterly exhibitions where students could share their learning journeys. Each exhibition has requirements based on the student's grade level and the status of their individual project work. Exhibitions offer students the opportunity to demonstrate their accountability for all facets of the Learning Plan. Parents, other students, advisors, mentors, and others attend and provide specific feedback. This type of demonstrable learning renders the influence of new apps like ChatGPT irrelevant.

Big Picture Learning Australia (BPLA) took the concept of authentic assessment to a new level with the introduction of the International Big Picture Learning Credential (IBPLC). Under the brilliant leadership of BPLA's Co-Founder and CEO Viv White and in collaboration with Elliot, they developed a personalized form of assessment that has now been accepted by over 40% of Australia's universities, including the prestigious University of Melbourne. It can also be used for entry into post-secondary trade schools and in lieu of résumés for work. The IBPLC is now being piloted in several U.S. states.

The IBPLC is similar to a digital portfolio reflecting a student's capacities, experiences, and qualities. It serves to level the playing field for diverse cultures, circumstances, and socio-economic status more fairly than exam-based certification systems. The IBPLC measures how you are smart, not how smart you are to specified outcomes. It is described below:

> The impetus is to put the "person" back into educational assessment so that young people exiting schooling do so with a rich, customized portrait of their abilities that offers meaningful, accessible information to end-users in the wider community, while allowing students significant agency in the way they are represented.
>
> As no two Big Picture students have the same interest-based learning pathway, a personalized approach to final-year assessment is required to provide a fair and balanced assessment that adequately portrays a student's distinctive learning, achievement, competencies, and potential.
>
> Unlike other forms of assessment, no attempt is made to rank or scale stu-

dents against each other. Their achievements are judged [by teachers, mentors and the students themselves] on demonstrations and observations of performance throughout their schooling against six specially constructed assessment frames in the areas of: Knowing How To Learn, Empirical Reasoning, Quantitative Reasoning, Social Reasoning, Communication, and Personal Qualities.

PROVEN RESULTS

Dennis and Elliot did not want to own schools. They wanted to show that educational transformation was possible using the principles I just discussed. They partnered with public school districts—in the most disadvantaged areas—to build new schools or operate within existing schools. Over the past several decades, studies have proven that these small, highly personalized schools—actively engaging with families and their surrounding communities—can transform lives and neighborhoods.

A longitudinal study of Big Picture schools' students and alumni, conducted by Boston College Lynch School of Education and Human Development,[3] found:

- **78%** of BPL students concurrently enrolled in community college classes while in high school

- **97%** of BPL students were admitted into two-year or four-year colleges

- **96%** of BPL alumni reported they were in touch with their high school advisors two or more years after graduation

- **74%** of BPL alumni who are working, and not enrolled in post–high school education, report securing a job through a contact made through one of their high school internships

- **49%** of BPL alumni participated in community service post-graduation

Conducted in academia, it is not surprising that the study views academic subject achievement and college persistence as highly valued. The high percentage of Big Picture students accepted to college can be deceptive, as all Big Picture students apply to college as part of their graduation requirements, but not all of them go on to attend. As noted before, most jobs—some very well paying—do not require a college degree.

Even more importantly, life satisfaction is highly correlated with the quality of relationships, and the Big Picture Learning model helps students *"develop the skills to build and maintain connections and forge relationships over time."* The study reported that students and alumni felt deeply connected to peers and adults and concluded that *"the Big Picture Learning model is extremely successful in meeting its stated goals of fostering positive relationships, helping students discover and pursue their interests, and promoting high school graduation and college entrance."*[4]

BIG PICTURE LEARNING MOVING FORWARD

After many years of tirelessly spearheading Big Picture Learning's efforts to show that educational transformation was possible, Dennis and Elliot recognized that, for the organization to continue to evolve, they needed to turn the reins over to a younger generation of leaders. In 2017, Andrew Frishman and Carlos, former teachers, advisors, and principals at Big Picture schools, became Co-Executive Directors under Elliot's mentorship.

After the transition, neither Dennis nor Elliot rested on their many laurels or retired. They both became actively engaged in new ventures that complemented and expanded upon their original mission. Before moving on, they authored books to share their philosophy and experience. Dennis (with Samantha Grabelle) wrote *The Big Picture: Education Is Everyone's Business*, and Elliot (with Charles Mojkowski) wrote *Leaving to Learn: How Out-of-School Learning Increases Student*

Engagement and Reduces Dropout Rates. Elliot also recently published *Learning to Leave: How Real-World Learning Transforms Education* with Scott Boldt.

Dennis went on to found College Unbound (CU) located on The Met campus to support working adult learners, including parents of students, who faced significant barriers to attending college. Using Big Picture Learning principles, CU helps returning adult learners achieve Bachelor's Degrees designed around an innovative, personalized, and interest or project-based curriculum model. Through Dennis' tenacity and persistence, CU is now a fully accredited college and expanding to other locations, including prisons, Native American reservations, and more.

Elliot turned his attention to developing the new forms, new ways, and new measures work of Big Picture Learning and has been instrumental in initiatives like BPLiving (related to student health and well-being), Harbor Freight Fellowship (related to hands-on learning), Project Insight (related to learning about eye care), and the IBPLC, as well as supporting others doing similar learner-centered work through-out the world. Elliot believes in the organization's "do-think-do" strategy of innovation and continues to push the boundaries of its design. I have the honor and privilege of partnering with him for his newest venture, B-Unbound, which I will describe in the next chapter.

Under the leadership of Carlos and Andrew, Big Picture Learning continues to evolve while focusing on its core mission of expanding the network of Big Picture schools. Their near-term agenda and long-term vision are focused on schools, innovation, and influence.

It is in the areas of innovation and influence that Carlos sees opportunities for change. He describes Big Picture Learning's role in a broader context:

Our work is not just at the school level, but also at the district and system leadership level, which is why we're leaning heavily into a variety of our different fellowship programs. We're working with school and system-level leaders that are not already part of our network to help us enable and set the conditions for these types of opportunities. It doesn't just have to be Big Picture schools, but truly learner-centered schools that allow for young people to learn and thrive outside of the school walls.

Carlos says, "*Our sweet spot has always been and continues to be the work with launching new schools and also helping shift and change practices in existing schools to be more learner-centered and equitable.*" When I asked him if he has seen a pendulum shift toward learner-centered models, Carlos replied that there is "*more of an openness to this type of learning and teaching. We are as big and full as we have ever been. So while we are bursting at the seams, the challenge continues to be that we are pushing up against a larger system and the conventional structures around it like reporting and testing.*"

He goes on to say that:

The conversation still exists around this college-for-all mentality. Poorer, underserved communities and communities of color see college as a way out. While I believe all parents want their children to be happy in what they decide to do, many believe that a degree gives them more options. While we don't fully subscribe to that thinking and know what the data shows, we understand why that mentality exists.

A search for a different approach to public education—one that incorporated social justice and equitable opportunities—was what drew Andrew to Big Picture Learning in the first place. After getting a Master's in Biology and teaching in private schools, Andrew entered a Master's in Teaching program at Brown University and worked in public schools while earning his degree. He was frustrated that he hadn't seen a school that worked well for students.

Just as he graduated, he attended an event about school innovation in Providence. Various principals and teachers stood up and talked about their schools, as well as a high school kid named Andy. Andy talked about attending four public and private schools between seventh and tenth grade and how he hated them all. His parents found out about The Met, and an advisor came to his home and asked about what he was interested in. When he said that he liked hanging out with his friends and talking about what they were going to be like fifty years from now, the advisor said, *"It sounds like you are interested in developmental psychology."* Andy didn't know what that was, so when he started at the school, he did some informational interviews with developmental psychology professors. He learned that he was more interested in anthropology, so he got an internship at the anthropology museum and put together an exhibit of toys and games of pre-colonial Native Americans.

Andy's story made an impact on Andrew. He remembers,

> *I don't know how you take a kid who is repeatedly disengaged and kicked out of schools and [get him to create] exhibits and do advanced anthropological stuff. So I walked up to him and his advisor after he talked and said I don't know what this is, but I want to be a part of it. I am going to come apply. I have a science degree and know it is hard to get science teachers. I want in.*

Andrew has been there ever since. He and Carlos understand what they are up against and are committed to the work they do alongside an exceptional team of dedicated professionals. Andrew describes the task of transforming education as follows:

> *It is phenomenally hard and difficult work to do and to do well. It is very intense because it is relentlessly intimate. It is emotionally both draining and recharging. It's like that line, "the toughest job you'll ever love." It's not less work or more work than conventional teaching. It's just different. It's totally different work.*
>
> *The difference between a Big Picture school and a conventional school is really about power. The teacher in a conventional school decides what gets taught and has a red correction pen. The kids are literally and figuratively sitting in rows facing you. When you shift to a Big Picture school, you're now an equal sitting around a round table, and your job is not to know all the content. Within a week of a kid being at an internship, they know a lot more than you do about whatever it is they are doing. You're a learning facilitator. It's just a totally different power. It's a collective collaborative based on "we" instead of "I." One of the most flattering things we have been accused of is that we are a youth development program disguised as a school.*

111

The thing that I always come back to with Big Picture is that if you find something you are really interested in, that you can do in the real world and connect with adults, that's what matters. That's what Big Picture is about from the beginning to the end—interest-driven, real-world learning. Our future is that we want more of that to happen. Who are the young people who don't get those opportunities, and how could we help them get that? How can we make that happen regardless of the type of school? It's a movement we are building. We are going to try lots of emergent pieces.

With compulsory attendance and guaranteed financial support through tax dollars or private investment, schools have had little motivation to adapt to the changes surrounding them. The layers of programs and testing mandates geared toward an outmoded economy have made them unable to respond to our rapidly transforming world. As previously noted, district and school leaders are stretched thin as they cope with all the responsibilities placed on schools—childcare, nutrition, mental health, security, sports, career, technical classes, and more—and so often have difficulty focusing on possibilities. These issues, plus political bureaucracies that can remove a Big Picture school, present headwinds to the wide adoption of the Big Picture Learning model and other schools like it.

As parents, we can play a role by working with schools and districts to encourage this type of learning ecosystem for our children. With so many hoops and layers to jump through, this endeavor is not for the faint of heart, but if we believe in the possibility of transforming public schools, it's worth it.

———

CHAPTER 6

WHAT IF ALL CHILDREN COULD B-UNBOUND?

You never change things by fighting the existing reality. To change something, build a new model that makes the existing model obsolete.

—Richard Buckminster Fuller

When Kate and Marisa asked me to join them in founding a new film company, Straight Up Impact, I agreed on the condition that I could pursue initiatives under our umbrella that would provide opportunities for people to participate in creating tangible change. While I believed in the power of good filmmaking to create awareness, evoke emotion, and promote conversation, I felt we had a responsibility to harness this energy and transform it into action.

The original idea was to list organizations and resources under each category where people could get involved if they chose, but these resources proved more difficult than originally thought since so many of the "solutions" are fed through the already overburdened systems we were highlighting. We were especially excited to have education icon Sir Ken Robinson and his daughter, also named Kate, join us as executive producers of our education film. We were looking forward to discussing potential resources based on his vast industry experience, but sadly, Sir Ken unexpectedly passed away during the filming. This was a huge loss for all concerned, personally and professionally.

Our education film highlighted the personal story of a teenager,

Mackenzie, who bravely shared her all-too-common experience of despair while trying to achieve the academic and sports accolades necessary for college admissions. The isolation and shame created by the continual comparison and competition took a toll on her mental health and well-being. All of us, including the film crew, were deeply impacted by her relatable perspective.

After the film shoot wrapped, I knew we had to do more than highlight resources for those experiencing crisis. I began to think about Viktor Frankl's work with suicidal patients. Although he listened to what made them want to end their lives, he was particularly interested in what made them want to live. His logotherapy theory focuses on dignity, strengths, and the responsibility to contribute our uniqueness to the world around us. Rather than concentrating resources on the crisis interventions available (although needed), I wanted to address preventing the distress in the first place by creating conditions and environments that promote well-being. These conditions and environments are found in relational communities where each person is known and respected, not in standardized systems designed to process people through to a designated output.

Although there were some isolated examples, it was hard to find a large organization that was actively engaged in this community-based approach in multiple geographic areas. I had written blogs about breaking down school walls to let students out into the community, but my research had not found many examples where a large group of students was able to direct their own explorations. The filming of Mackenzie's story inspired the idea for a community-based initiative that promoted youth voices in exploration and peer-to-peer sharing.

Trevor Davis, Kate's husband and a good friend of the Robinson family, reached out to Sir Ken's daughter Kate Robinson to ask if she knew of any community-based organizations in the U.S. that we could partner with. She suggested we talk with Sir Ken's good friend, Elliot Washor, the co-founder of Big Picture Learning. Since I was familiar with Big Picture Learning through Carlos, I commented to Trevor that we were looking to partner with a community-based organization, not a certain type of school. I wasn't sure that Elliot could really help us. Was I ever wrong!

It turns out that Elliot had been trying for years to expand Big Picture Learning's approach into communities. He knew that the slow, laborious process of working through schools was not going to help the large number of youth in desperate need of opportunity and hope. He had already developed a community-based program called Outlearners that created the infrastructure necessary to expand the possibilities available to all young people regardless of whether or not they attended school. It was, in essence, Big Picture Learning without the school.

Outlearners complemented and supplemented formal schooling but was not a state or school district–run organization—no membership forms to be filled out or qualifications to be met. It would reach beyond the barriers and regulations of traditional career and technical education programs to open up access to work and career opportunities. He came close to getting his Outlearners concept started in Brockton, Massachusetts, but the funding was never allocated.

After our initial group call, Elliot sent us information about Outlearners, and I couldn't believe the alignment of our missions as I read the following:

> *This is about relationships—being well-attached through one's personal interests and motivations—and putting young people in charge of their choices and their destinies, allowing their personal agency to shine through by getting them with the right people in the right places and situations at the right time. As one young person put it during a recent focus group session, to join, "all you have to do is walk in." And walking in is a key Outlearners requirement. Young people must choose to come, not be placed there by a social service agency or workforce development program.*
>
> *Outlearners is not a treatment program, not a remediation. Rather, its focus is prevention. Based on our research, no other program in the U.S. responds to the*

challenges our young people face in their efforts to build social capital with and through their interests and achieve social mobility.

For over twenty years, Big Picture Learning schools have successfully brought students from the inside to the outside where they connect with adults around their interests. Now as a way to scale our best practices, Outlearners will work from the outside to the inside, with adult [guides] supporting young people to make productive connections around each young person's interest. These [guides] will connect youth to people doing the real work—crafts and tradespeople, small business people, professionals, media companies, and community organizations.

Outlearners is a starting place but different from a place that tells young people what they must do, where, and when. Instead, Outlearners will braid together already existing work in schools and connect with youth who are not initially enrolled but can be supported in ways that make sense to them by connecting back in through their interests to people and organizations they want to be connected to. Many of these young people have already left or are very disengaged, and now they are coming back in, but this time someone is making their pathways the pathway.

Within a few hours of reviewing the information, I called Elliot and told him, *"Let's do this!"* I sold some of my investments and donated the funds to start what would become B-Unbound. Straight Up Impact was interested in complementing Outlearners with a peer-to-peer community where youth could support each other and share their stories through podcasts, videos, art, and more. We agreed that the initiative would be operated by Big Picture Learning, and I would devote time and energy to helping build it as a co-founder. The return on my investment, although not financial, has been substantial and among the most rewarding things I have ever done.

Our first call with Elliot was on January 15, 2021, and by mid-February, the operations team was in place to start building the platform. Big Picture Learning's Anthonette Peña was named the B-Unbound program director. The platform was built utilizing the ImBlaze software (discussed in the previous chapter), but unlike ImBlaze, whose database of mentors is often proprietary to schools, the B-Unbound database is built and shared by all participants in a community. In this way, social capital is not confined to certain zip codes or entities.

B-Unbound offers a life apprenticeship similar to how children learned alongside adults in communities throughout most of human evolution. The school model we know today is a fairly modern invention. It was developed about 150 years ago during the industrial age and reflected the economy of the time. Programs like B-Unbound get youth out of abstract studies and into relevant, real-world learning.

B-Unbound is an initiative powered by Big Picture Learning in collaboration with Straight Up Impact.

Because B-Unbound is not restricted to school-age students, we call young people (14–24) "Youth Navigators" and adults looking to navigate their way to new possibilities "Adult Navigators." B-Unbound runs parallel to school systems and is available to youth who attend any type of school (public, private, homeschool) or no school at all. It is available to those who have left high school or dropped out of college as well as those who have graduated and are looking to re-evaluate their area of focus.

The role of an advisor in B-Unbound is called "Co-Navigator," reflecting their guide-on-the-side position. This intermediary position provides critical support to Navigators and is often missing in traditional internship programs. The Navigator is in the driver's seat, the one who is choosing the direction and responsible for the investment of time and energy.

"Supportive Adults" are the experienced partners in the community who Navigators connect with around their interests. These partners can take many forms, including mentors, coaches, skill-based trainers, or informational interviewees. They can be virtual or in-person and vary depending on their time availability and desire to participate, and roles range from hosting workplace tours to shadow days to skill-building apprenticeships. Interested Supportive Adults with little time but a desire to help can play the role of "Connector" by leveraging their own personal and professional networks to find individuals engaged in specific interests that Navigators may be seeking. All these roles energize and support the unique explorations of each youth.

In B-Unbound, interests are not restricted to those that could create future work; they involve the intuitive pull toward curiosities. They can relate to passions or an interest in solving problems Navigators see in their communities. Following interests can lead to a new field or discovery. For example, someone could be interested in deep-sea fishing and, through that experience, see all the plastic in the ocean and decide to develop a new solution.

While policymakers, administrators, and educators argue over whether charter schools are better than traditional public schools or whether school vouchers are more beneficial than funding districts, we at B-Unbound focus on promoting decision-making capabilities and fostering a sense of responsibility. We are working toward building a community that honors the dignity of the individual, expands potential, and promotes well-being. To the extent taxpayer funding is necessary for schooling, it should be used to facilitate an individual's pursuit of interests, experiences, and relationships.

Because the parent company, Big Picture Learning, is a not-for-profit, funding for B-Unbound mostly comes from donations and grants. In an effort to create a more consistent revenue source, there are also nominal fees for licensing and training.

Focusing on a specific type of school or funding method misses the central challenge—the devaluing of human uniqueness and potential within mechanistic systems. All types of schools (public, private, charter) and funding protocols tend to utilize the same outcome metrics (grades, test scores) and comparisons that are illegitimate to begin with. The wide variety of human intelligences and their unique compositions within each person cannot be fully understood or measured and certainly don't provide an accurate basis for comparison. The litmus test for all types of schools ought to relate to whether they create the opportunities and conditions necessary to 1) promote dignity and respect; 2) elevate relational connection; and 3) encourage responsible contributions based on meaningful pursuits.

THE ART OF THE PIVOT

Unlike school-related internships or projects assigned by adults, Navigators learn to self-assess their progress and discern whether their interest, relationships, and practice are providing them with meaningful fulfillment or whether it is time to pivot. They learn to follow their intuitive guidance. B-Unbound has no time restrictions, which allows for the fluid navigation of their explorations. If they stay only within the confines of our linear education system, they do not learn one of the essential skills they will need for life, the art of the pivot.

By *pivot*, I mean the ability to look around at possibilities and make the decision to change course. This could be upskilling to a new aspect of current work or changing directions to pursue other more meaningful work. It applies to our children's personal lives as well. As they progress through life's stages and encounter different people and experiences, their perspectives, values, and priorities will change. They will need to change course to respond to these shifts.

Pivoting is happening all around us as our global economy is undergoing a dramatic transformation driven by technology. The old white-collar/blue-collar model has been redefined, and well-paying new-collar industries have been added to the mix. We have to refrain from filtering everything through the lens of what we understood to be true in the past because this will only hinder our children's ability to move forward into this new era.

New types of training programs, often run by companies, are emerging, and the opportunity to work remotely has expanded where people can choose to live. The experience of being locked down during the COVID-19 pandemic created a collective pause and prompted many people to shift their priorities.

I call it the *art of the pivot* because there are no set rules. Decisions are unique to the individual and the situations they find themselves in. Unfortunately, we have trained our children to fit into structured programs rather than having them learn to navigate their own way. When they don't have a rigid structure, they can often feel stuck and not know where to begin.

I have seen this with many of the kids I know, including my own, and hear it from parents who express concern and frustration. There is a lack of responsibility for the direction of their own lives and a lack of confidence in their ability to pursue what they would like to do (if they can even identify it). When they ultimately graduate and go into the real world, they are unfamiliar with how it operates. I see this as a direct reflection of the confined silos they have been raised in and the compliant manner they have been required to adopt. They often wait for someone else to tell them what to do next. They expect that life will be like school, where they receive timely feedback and progress in a straight line toward project completion or grade-level advancement.

In life, feedback is not always concrete or timely. People don't always respond or provide guidance. Our children will get turned down for jobs or not be accepted to programs of their choice. I tell my daughters and the kids I mentor it is just *"a communication signal that this path is not the right one"* or *"it's not the right time—pivot and go another direction."* Rejection provides directional information; it is not a determinant of worthiness.

Knowing when to pivot requires that our children learn to listen to their conscience and cultivate a network of people they can turn to for support. The agility required of life is essential to their futures as new industries—and opportunities—are forming as fast as others are dying. Our children are likely to experience multiple transition periods related to work, either by their choice or because of their employer's transforming needs.

A college degree today is typically not enough to power earnings throughout a lifetime. Even those students graduating with high-paying science, technology, engineering, and math (STEM) degrees aren't always reaping long-term financial benefits and job security. A Harvard study showed a more than 50% decline in STEM earnings within the first decade of working, and by the end of ten years, many were no longer in the field.[1] Technological advancements are moving too quickly. Continual reskilling and upskilling are required regardless of educational attainment.

New economies have emerged in the past few decades that are

powering the shift away from industrialized systems; these include the freelance or solopreneur economy and the sharing economy. Our children may choose or be required to navigate two or three avenues of income for financial stability. They may weave in and out of them or have all three going at the same time. The value of time over money seems to be different for younger generations than it was for my generation, and this may be playing a role in the large number of unfilled corporate jobs currently available.

Our children will likely be most successful if they have a skill to offer, the ability to market themselves on platforms related to that skill, and a network of friends and professional affiliations who can offer help finding work. Navigating their way in the twenty-first century will depend on knowing how to: 1) get a job; 2) create a job based on a specific skill; and 3) utilize owned or made assets for income.

When I say *skill*, I am not just talking about a trade or professional certification. I am also talking about caregiving, childcare, gardening, culinary, art, and other talents needed to support our communities. They are often dismissed in our narrow definition of skills related only to economic output. The sharing economy has created an opportunity to barter and trade our talents using community-based tech platforms for connection.

Learning when and how to pivot will help our children gain the agility necessary to co-create the lives they dream of. Whereas my generation had to be tied to a full-time job with a single company, often in a single location for fixed hours, my daughters' generation has the freedom to choose a different path. People often lament that it is less secure, but the reality is that a corporate job is not secure either. Someone could work for ten or twenty years for a single company and still get a pink slip terminating their employment. Workers are viewed as expendable if that is what the bottom line requires. Those with the skills necessary to pivot at such a time and who have cultivated a broad network of relationships will have a better chance of facing the challenge head-on. Without those skills, their fragility will make them vulnerable and dependent.

FILLING THE GAPING HOLE

B-Unbound plays a valuable role in helping to fill the gaping hole found in all types of education systems (public and private)—it connects youth to real-world learning. This is critical in applying theoretical information to actual practice. Experience is essential to learning. Schools focus on determining *what* they think all students need to know. Just like the unwritten road rules that are incredibly important to driving, in life, the *who*, *how*, and *why* are arguably more important.

WHO

As stated previously, the majority of jobs are found through knowing people or being recommended to someone. This is increasingly critical as most jobs are not posted. Many companies are incentivizing employees to help find the necessary skilled individuals they need for open positions. The increasing number of skilled freelancers rely on project connections to get additional work rather than finding new work through posted offerings. I saw this in action on the film set when the director recommended a cinematographer who referred an editor, and so on. Nothing was posted.

Julia Freeland Fisher, Director of Education Research at the Christensen Institute,[2] describes the importance of what she calls *relationship mapping*: "*The research is clear: positive and diverse relationships in students' lives can buffer risk, boost academic performance and persistence, and ultimately expand professional opportunities. The opposite is also true: a dearth of connections can have dire consequences for students' well-being, academic success, and eventual career prospects."*[3]

Once someone's innate curiosities and interests are identified and a specific area is chosen to start, the importance of social networking comes to the forefront. Youth and Adult Navigators begin by thinking of existing, trusted relationships they already have related to their family, neighborhood, community organizations, school, or work. These offer the starting point from which to build and leverage new relationships.

This process of relationship mapping is an invaluable life skill for our children to learn. Once they understand how to do this, they will use it throughout their lives. Fisher says, *"Relationship mapping can help students connect the dots between where they are, where they want to go, and who they already know that can help get them there. Sometimes networking isn't about meeting new people, but having new conversations with people you already know." Who* our children know is more than a social media connection; it is also about who knows them.

As Supportive Adults commit to joining the B-Unbound database, they can be available to Navigators who share their same interests. They are learners and co-creators alongside Navigators with the added benefit of being able to share their years of experience. The database is built from the bottom up in each community, and any Supportive Adults who will be working with Navigators under 18 are subject to background checks. As the database gets filled, social capital and opportunities become accessible to more individuals across a broad geographic area.

Huge shifts are taking place, and new opportunities are emerging that may not fall into our current predefined "career clusters" that career and technical education (CTE) programs promote. In many ways, the term *career* is a misnomer since technology and new ways of working are shaking up traditional fields of study. Schools cannot keep up with the rapidly evolving workplace, and the disconnection is continually widening. CTE programs should be community-based, not school-based so they can keep up with real-time changes and quickly adapt as new opportunities emerge.

In our busy world, we focus more on tasks than on relationships, but nurturing a relationship requires time and attention. The B-Unbound program and platform provide opportunities for meaningful connections around interests. It encourages multigenerational relationships and networks of support that can last a lifetime and change the lives of all involved.

HOW

We are human beings, not programmable robots. We tend to go a mile wide and an inch deep with subjects rather than allowing students to dive further into their areas of interest and *"learn by doing,"* as John Dewey advocated. We ignore the valuable role that multiple types of intelligences play in the vibrant fabric of communities and insist that everyone have the same kind of intelligence, even though it is humanly impossible. We have missed leveraging the tacit knowledge inherent in everyone—that is, the inner knowing and aptitude some people have for certain things like music, science, art, math, and more.

We delude ourselves into thinking that if we are teaching it to them, they must be learning. This is not the case since there are so many variables that go into true learning (versus memorization for tests), including relevance, interest, relationships, safety, environment, and nutrition, to name a few. Learning is a part of being human and happens in all environments, not just in schools.

Getting good at something takes practice, and hands-on engagement is how we develop skills, particularly when we have the support of others. Family traditions and recipes are passed on in this manner, and it is why apprenticeships are often successful for skill-specific workforces. The world is changing so fast that our children need to be interacting in the real world to see the possibilities and take advantage of the opportunities. They need to be unbound.

Wouldn't it be better to let our children figure out what they are interested in and explore it before committing so much time and money to college? College is now an "if" and "when" option—*if* the student needs it for their particular interest or field of study and *when* they decide to go is no longer tied to a certain age. College degrees can be attained at any stage of life and in a variety of formats.

Without real-life experience, our children, confined to systems, become like tree saplings that are staked when they are put in the ground and never have the stakes removed. These saplings don't develop the deep root system necessary to tap into vital underground resources or the trunk strength required to withstand strong winds and rain; they can topple easily. We have the power to ensure our children develop the strengths necessary to weather whatever life brings them.

Despite my best efforts, I found differing levels of willingness among my daughters to embrace real-world learning experiences during high school and college. Few of their peers were doing it. I insisted that my daughters were involved in something outside of the school-related bubble so they could see themselves in a different context. They volunteered regularly, and two of them worked part-time jobs, making minimum wage in food service (the nature of my other daughter's interests regrettably always interfered with her ability to commit time to a job).

Emily found her career as a speech therapist as a direct result of her experiences outside of school. While in high school, she volunteered as a counselor at an annual summer camp that paired students with special needs children. She loved being with these children and continued as a staff member even after graduation. Emily knew she wanted to find a career in a related field, so in her last semester of high school, she did an internship at a therapeutic horse-riding center that offered occupational, physical, and speech therapy. Because she had already applied to college and had declared a major, she had to switch once she started, and luckily there was space available in the speech therapy department. (Imagine if, early in high school, students could explore internships before applying to college.) She is now working professionally and is very fulfilled in her chosen field.

Although I intuitively knew the importance of placing my children in the driver's seat out in the real world, engaged in their interests, relationships, and practice, it was not a social norm in our community. Like many kids today, their comfort zone is inside the bubble. This sometimes created headwinds to my efforts. They didn't want to be different from their friends who were following the academic path. This is understandable given the silos we have created, but launching into adulthood from this comfort zone is hard, and the necessary transition can be extremely anxiety-producing for many kids.

B-Unbound facilitates the understanding and deepening of skills and practices. Wanting to learn something and having someone to learn with are key components that open a world of possibilities for our children. And if they are doing so in a community with their peers, they won't feel unusual and insecure about their choices.

WHY

As human beings, we are motivated to find meaning in our lives. Our creative contributions to work or deeds performed; our experiences with art, nature, or the love of another; as well as the attitude we take toward unavoidable suffering can give us meaning and purpose. As repeatedly stated, meaning is specific to an individual, and as such, we are the only ones who can truly respond to the situations and events in our lives. We shape the world around us, and it shapes us as we evolve together.

We cannot give meaning or create it for someone else as we so often try to do in our society, especially with our children. In doing this, we frustrate their personal pursuit of meaning, the responsibility they have to make the most of their own lives, and the beneficial role meaning plays in their health and wellness.

Although meaning is a necessary component of our lives, fate always plays a role. We cannot escape pain, guilt, or death; we can only respond to them. They give us the opportunity to transform ourselves. Suffering is not required to find meaning, but it is often through pain and struggles that we grow and learn. Guilt allows us to decide to do things differently in the future. And it is through our acceptance of death that we can decide to value whatever time we have and contribute ourselves as we are called to do.

Many programs outline steps to health but ignore the fact that people need a reason to want to care for themselves. While sleep, eating well, exercising, and avoiding harmful substances are all important, they keep the focus on us and a checklist. This to-do mindset promotes an existence, not true living. As Friedrich Nietzsche said, *"He who has a why to live can bear almost any how."*

Why is the engine that fuels the pursuit of meaning. It keeps us strong when obstacles emerge. Meaningful tension is essential, and the struggle to persevere propels us forward in life. Our cultural search for equilibrium through meditation and other de-stressing methods often provides a counterbalance to the busyness and meaninglessness of our lives; it does not always propel us forward to becoming who we want to be.

From a young age, our children gravitate toward specific interests and curiosities—they are intuitively drawn to certain things and certain people. Each has a potential contribution to make and an irreplaceable role to play in the evolution of humanity. We have limited this potential in our standardized systems of living.

B-Unbound creates conditions that inspire hope, courage, and confidence in pursuing meaning. It helps the Navigator listen to their intuitive guidance— their conscience—and explore with the support of others. As Rumi said, *"As you start to walk on the way, the way appears."*

SHIFTING RESPONSIBILITIES

Our institutions are failing. The industrialized and digital approaches to enhancing human life have, in many ways, contributed to the opposite—just look at our fragmented society, the environmental crisis, and the epidemic of anxiety and depression. As we wake up to the reality of modern life, we find ourselves at a fork in the road. Do we continue to place unfair burdens onto school systems to prepare our children for life, or do we shift some of this responsibility back to ourselves and our communities?

We cannot manufacture a fulfilling life for our children in a mass-production model. Peter Gray notes, *"The pressure and continuous monitoring and judgments from adults, coupled with the loss of freedom to follow their own interests and solve their own problems, results in anxiety, depression, and general dissatisfaction with life."*[4] Our way of living is not conducive to human flourishing.

Over thirty-five years ago, Edward L. Deci and Richard M. Ryan developed Self-Determination Theory, which emphasizes the importance of intrinsic motivation in performance and happiness (that is, being motivated by our internal desires and decision-making capabilities). Extrinsic motivators such as rewards and punishments (demanded from outside sources) do not create long-term satisfaction or a desire to perform. Satisfaction relates to the deeply personal search for meaning.

Rather than addressing the root cause of our distress and working to change it, we are an interventionist society that spends most of its time and effort putting a band-aid on the problem. We want the pill, therapy, program, or device that will make it go away. We keep pulling people out of the river and don't address the upstream issues that are throwing them into the river in the first place. Intervention is needed, of course, but we have to put equal or more effort into prevention to shift the cultural tide. The contributions we each make play an essential role in this shift.

B-Unbound is focused on the structural underpinnings of our society that have lost sight of our children's basic psychological needs for autonomy, competence, and relatedness. It provides a platform and a program that shifts responsibility from dependence on mechanistic institutions to relational communities of support for individual contributions and human thriving.

With the mission to free our children to navigate their own way to a meaningful life, the principles of B-Unbound can be utilized by individual parents, groups of parents, or organizations. As I tried to do when raising my children, we can do this in our individual homes, but I believe the African proverb: "*If you want to go fast, go alone. If you want to go far, go together.*" If possible, it is better to go together.

B-UNBOUND PILOTS

There are twenty-four B-Unbound pilots in community-based organizations such as Boys & Girls Clubs, maker spaces, community resource centers, and apprentice-training hubs in several states (as of March 2023). We have also partnered with the Sweetwater Union High School District in San Diego for their after-school program and even started working with adult education programs in California and Washington.

Two of our partner pilots, Bluedoor Community[5] and Habitat for Aviation,[6] offer particularly innovative approaches to community-based educational support. Both were started by amazing women determined to respect the unique human potential in every young person.

Bluedoor Community is located in Auburn, California, a small rural area near Sacramento. It was started by a homeschooling mom, Katie Burns, who wanted to enrich the different learning interests of her children. Her son became interested in physics, and she reached out to a fellow homeschooling dad and asked if he would teach her son physics if she taught his child biology. This soon grew to other homeschooling parents offering to teach their particular area of interest, and the Bluedoor Community was born.

The co-op arrangement expanded and evolved into a resource center for homeschool and charter-affiliated families, offering a variety of classes without a preset program structure. Katie rented space from a local church, formed a nonprofit in 2018, and recently moved into a campus facility. To date, they have over 450 students and are expanding to include offerings to a wide variety of age groups in the community, including seniors. Their website highlights the following:

Bluedoor is not a school; rather, it is a nonprofit that organizes and schedules classes taught by high-quality educators. Each teacher at Bluedoor believes in the value of every child and works to introduce opportunities to students through dynamic classes. Students in K–12th grade are provided classes covering all core subjects and many enrichments in one location. All Bluedoor teachers are committed to providing classes that get students involved, incorporate real-world skills, and inspire students to reach for success. Bluedoor teachers work with charter schools to give families flexible options for paying for classes that meet state standards through engaging methods.

Bluedoor facilitates social engagement by incorporating dances, spirit days (such as crazy hair day, etc.), and a yearbook for members of their community. There are week-long breaks called Bluedoor Outdoor, where families can individually or collectively "leave to learn." The outings organized by Bluedoor are open to all family members, including grandparents and siblings.

Bluedoor partnered with B-Unbound to manage and expand internship opportunities for their 140 high schoolers. They formed a B-Unbound Club for interested youth. This club acts similarly to an advisory in a Big Picture school, providing a launching pad for youth to share and explore ideas and interests along with their peers. Bluedoor will eventually expand its B-Unbound real-world learning opportunities to include any youth (14–24) living in the area. As it is not bound to a specific type of school or any school at all for that matter, it provides a valuable resource to the community. They are a powerful contributor to creating a new approach to how children learn and grow.

Beth White, a former teacher and fierce advocate for hands-on learning, recently started Habitat for Aviation in Vermont, which is now a B-Unbound hub. She has worked with Big Picture Learning in various capacities for many years. She also worked in different types of schools where she found herself challenging the standardized approach to students and getting herself into hot water with administrators. Her experiences fueled her desire to offer hands-on alternatives that could be credited as school. This led her to get a doctorate in educational leadership and policy studies at the University of Vermont. She says:

> My dissertation was around research experiences for undergraduates. One of the most powerful pieces of data that came out of that was they got the most out of what we called the brown bag lunch talks. The undergraduates realized that when research professors shared their journey, they realized, wow, it wasn't linear. For example, this one professor took time off to be a dog walker and still became a scientist. It demystified the pathway to doing what makes your heart sing.

Early in her career, Beth worked with Big Picture Learning at The Met and became deeply committed to the principles they represent. She describes herself as a country girl, which is why she couldn't stay in Providence and returned to Vermont. Five years ago, she was reading the memoir *West with the Night* by Beryl Markham and became inspired to learn to fly. While training for her pilot license, a former teacher who was ill learned of her interest. When he passed away, he left her his airplane and hangar. This opened up new opportunities for Beth.

As she is raising capital for the renovation of her Habitat for Aviation building, her program is temporarily based out of a local Vermont airport hangar owned by George Coy's company, Fly Vermont. They have five planes that young people can learn to fly and service. Students earn credit and stipends under B-Unbound's Harbor Freight Fellowship program.

Beth tells the story of a student, Ian, who was badly harassed in middle school, as a way to highlight how our current systems hinder real-world learning. Ian became a Harbor Freight Fellow working alongside his mentor, George, fixing airplanes. He earned a $500 stipend, which was enough to buy a broken-down J3 Kitten airplane to restore. He was fully engaged in the process. As Ian entered high school, the system's demands continued to limit his experiences. When a local company offered a public information night about a robotics program, he was unable to attend because he had too much homework to do. Beth says, *"How sad is that? This was a robotics thing presented by an aerospace company, and it couldn't count as school."*

There are so many of these examples that keep her motivated. One of her goals is to expand opportunities in aviation for women and underserved populations. Another student, Julie, is also a Harbor Freight Fellow studying aviation mechanics. In school, she always felt average, but her mentor George describes her as exceptional. He shows her how to do something once, and she gets it. *"She never had feedback like that her whole life, and she is 17 years old,"* comments Beth.

The role mentors play is more than work-related. When Julie wanted to spend her stipend getting her gerbil's teeth fixed, Beth asked her when she herself had been to a dentist. It had been six years. *"So now it's more than fixing airplanes,"* Beth says. *"Mentors can become that person you go to in order to have those important conversations about life."* Beth's advocacy has created new opportunities for youth in her community.

MOVING FORWARD

Our biggest barrier to B-Unbound's widespread adoption within organizations is the difficulty in shifting cultural norms. Organizational frameworks are typically designed for measures and output, not the nurturing of individuals. These frameworks are geared toward specific training and standardized reporting, not pulling out human potential or encouraging outside relationships and exploration. Developing advisory-type Navigator groups within these organizations can help provide a base for human-scale support as they learn to venture out together.

Societal shifts require the telling of a new story of possibility. We have a cultural narrative that all children must be processed through the school system and go to college to be worthy in our society and to achieve financial viability. This reminds me of the folktale "The Emperor's New Clothes"—we are ignoring a very visible problem. We are all pretending that this is working for the vast majority of children when we can all see that it is not. Look around. Although it might be beneficial to a few, it is not working for the masses as promised.

Cultural anthropologist Margaret Mead was once asked what she thought was the first sign of civilization. Rather than saying fire or tools, she described a broken femur that had healed. Civilization, in her view, began when people looked out for each other; when they came together to care for and nurture each other.[7] Communities are vital to our survival and ability to thrive.

B-Unbound offers an opportunity to free youth from the confinement of top-down structures that predetermine possibilities based on historic economic roles. It expands possibilities, and therefore human potential, through engagement with the real world of people, nature, ideas, challenges, and more. It encourages the pursuit of meaning as each youth follows their intuitive pull toward interests and curiosities and becomes interconnected with adults and peers in their community who can support them. Most of all, it promotes responsibility for themselves and to others as each recognizes the valuable, unique, and irreplaceable contribution they can make to the future.

Parents can play a pivotal role in promoting youth-driven, adult-supported exploration by encouraging organizations to adopt a new perspective. But we cannot rely on organizations alone. We need to reinforce the necessary values and priorities at home. Riding alongside a youth learning to navigate their own way is at the same time a harrowing and exhilarating adventure—and one of the most fulfilling experiences in life.

———

PART III

WHERE WE CAN GO

CHAPTER 7

WHO IS BUILDING THE NEW INFRASTRUCTURE?

When a flower doesn't bloom, you fix the environment in which it grows, not the flower.

—Alexander den Heijer

As I awakened to new perspectives through my experiences raising my children, going back to college, and starting my blog, I began meeting inspiring people who recognize the need for a cultural pivot and are working hard to do something about it. In this chapter, I can only highlight a small number whom I have interacted with personally. They all give me hope for the future and motivate me to continue my efforts. Each person's unique contribution is creating a new infrastructure of roads and bridges for our children.

I talk about my mission to anyone who will listen, and it is amazing the doors that have opened. My family, friends, and acquaintances often suggest introductions. I continue to trust when I feel a strong intuitive pull and respond to these suggestions when they are aligned. I do not set specific goals to drive toward; I just keep following the bouncing ball of opportunity as it comes. Uncertainty is the only certainty there really is.

DIXON CHIBANDA

A few months after I started working with Kate and Marisa on Straight Up Impact, I was at a family event, talking with my brother-in-law, Bill Roy. I explained my interest in the power of film and the need for quality content that raised awareness about social issues, nourished the soul, and provided hope. Bill, a successful entrepreneur in finance and technology, mentioned that he, too, was unexpectedly involved in a film production for similar reasons. Along with his filmmaker friend Graham Leader of SeaLion Films, he had become a producer on a documentary about the Friendship Bench,[1] a community-based program started in Zimbabwe that trained grandmothers to treat depression.

I couldn't believe it! A few months before, my friend Margarita had sent me the TED Talk by the founder of the Friendship Bench, Dr. Dixon Chibanda. It was one of the most impactful TED Talks I had ever seen, and its evidence-based approach showed what was possible through community engagement. I immediately offered to join Bill as an executive producer of the film.

Once again, my interest was not in the film production itself but in the opportunities that the film could provide for spreading the concept of the Friendship Bench. I got to know Dixon through our production meetings, and as I learned his story, I became even more determined that it needed to be told. It shows what is possible when one person decides to contribute to needed change. His story, although not directly related to the educational system, shows the powerful impact of the kind of community support that I am advocating for in this book.

Dixon is one of 12 registered psychiatrists serving 16 million people in Zimbabwe, a country with the highest suicide and depression rates in Africa. The suicide of a young patient without the needed bus fare to reach him motivated him to re-evaluate the relationship between the healthcare system and the community. There were just not enough healthcare providers to address the magnitude of the distress being experienced by people in his country. He recognized the need to build local community support that was accessible to everyone in order to address the ever-growing rates of anxiety and depression.

Using his own money, he started the Friendship Bench in 2006 with fourteen grandmothers who lived in one of the hardest-hit communities. He taught them how to evaluate clients' mental health and implement evidence-based talk therapy. They, in turn, taught him about the importance of local culture and language, the healing power of empathy, and the need for proximate relationships.

The grandmothers challenged some of the mechanical approaches being applied to human beings by the healthcare system. As Grandmother Jack told Dixon, *"I don't jump into problem-solving therapy, but rather, the first thing I say is, 'I'm here for you. Would you like to share your story with me?'"* She advised, *"People are not machines; you must remove your medical hat and immerse yourself in the community and cultural thinking."*

Working together, they refined a prototype for the Friendship Bench to be delivered on strategically located community benches. Within six months, the 14 grandmothers had seen over 3,000 people. Clients considered at high risk of suicide were referred to a clinic, but most required one to six sessions on the bench.

Over 280,000 people have received treatment through Friendship Bench including tens of thousands in Malawi, Kenya, Vietnam, Canada, and other host countries (1st Quarter, 2023). To date, more than 2,000 grandmothers and other lay people have been trained, and the results are hard to ignore: **Clinical studies show a 78 to 80% reduction in depression symptoms.**[2] No prescription medication is needed, and the delivery costs are very inexpensive compared to standard mental health treatments offered through the healthcare system. Although the crisis is still overwhelming, the Friendship Bench is helping to stem the tide of those not needing acute care, relieving the burden placed on local healthcare clinics.

The Friendship Bench has evolved into training all types of lay people reflecting varied communities (men, LGBTQ+, youth), not just grandmothers. The meaningful work and relationships created have changed the lives of the Friendship Bench volunteers as well as their clients and communities.

To ensure that supportive infrastructure is established once clients leave the bench, they are introduced to peer-led support groups. These groups help build local relationships that can buffer against isolation and loneliness—major contributors to mental distress. In Africa, group members work together on income-producing endeavors, including weaving shopping baskets out of recycled plastic bags.

In the U.S., B-Unbound can provide a further opportunity to connect Friendship Bench circle group members to people in their communities. These relationships can relate to finding work, engaging in hobbies, exploring things they are curious about, or joining causes that matter to them. This expands their relational network of support.

As nice as it is to be in a safe group, it can create fragility and limit possibilities. Being at the edge of our comfort zone is where aliveness happens. Expressing our authentic selves, pursuing what matters to us, and interacting with people, ideas, and nature can help us discover meaning and purpose.

Dixon's 2017 TED Talk, "Why I Train Grandmothers to Treat Depression," has been viewed by millions as the theme of community engagement resonates across the globe. The documentary is due to be released in late 2023, and Dixon is writing a book about his experiences in developing the Friendship Bench. He and I are aligned in our hope to have a Friendship Bench within walking distance of anyone who needs it in every community. To this end, we are actively working together to find partners to pilot Friendship Benches in the U.S.

The weaving of these community networks of support is essential to the future of our society and the individuals within it. It is through these human-scale engagements that we can develop a sense of belonging, safety, and dignity. Mass production of human beings through systems—education, healthcare, foster care, social services, criminal justice—cannot achieve this because the sheer scale involved requires the reduction of the human to a category (such as student, worker, patient, and so on) as they are processed through. We have the power to change that. As Dixon's story shows, one person deciding to change the status quo can ripple across the globe.

LARGE-SCALE CHANGEMAKERS

One of the primary catalysts for my advocacy was Sir Ken Robinson. As I watched his iconic TED Talk, "Do Schools Kill Creativity?" I knew I wasn't alone. His subsequent talks and books continue to inspire me to this day. I was so excited when he and his daughter, Kate, joined our film team as executive producers and was devastated when he unexpectedly passed away before I had the opportunity to work with him.

I was first exposed to Sir Ken through a documentary film by director Vicki Abeles, a mother-turned-filmmaker. Vicki is a former attorney who describes her advocacy as follows:

My own awakening to the toxicity of the achievement race came the way it does to many parents: via years of trying to keep up with it. When my three kids were younger, our family spent weekends together, played in parks, visited museums, gathered around the table most nights for dinner.

But as my kids got older, their lives mutated into a state of busyness and stress that gave our home the air of a corporate command center. And I should know—I was a Wall Street attorney who saw her 12-year-old daughter working longer hours than I ever did for law school. I decided to pick up a camera to expose this silent epidemic of anxiety, depression, and disengagement that has infiltrated our schools, our lives, our culture, our society.

I had no filmmaking experience, so the project was quite an adventure. I drew from many years of working as an attorney to take a stand and become an advocate. But above all, my work has been propelled by the power of people coming together.

Vicki and I connected when my daughters' alternative elementary school hosted a screening of her groundbreaking documentary *Race to Nowhere: The Dark Side of American Achievement Culture*. Soon after, she was raising funds through Kickstarter for a follow-up film, *Beyond Measure: Schools at the Heart of Change*, which I participated in supporting. Vicki has gone on to found the organization Beyond the Race to Nowhere[3] to galvanize a movement of parents, teachers, school leaders, students, and more to advocate for healthier futures for all children, and she continues to make and promote films that challenge our societal narratives.

As I searched for ways to contribute, I came across another TED Talk, "Everything You Think You Know About Addiction Is Wrong" by British journalist and *New York Times* bestselling author Johann Hari.[4] In the talk, Johann highlighted the Rat Park experiment by Dr. Bruce Alexander,[5] which so powerfully illustrates the need for interconnectedness. In experiments on addiction conducted by other researchers, a single rat was placed in a solitary cage with two options for water, one plain and one with morphine. The rats in this situation chose the morphine water. But when Dr. Alexander experimented with putting rats in a large park-like setting full of other rats and the same water choices, the rats had much less appetite for the morphine water. Even rats who were previously addicted would stop drinking the morphine water when they entered the rat park. This further reinforces the importance of community and the negative impact of isolation and confinement.

Johann concluded his talk by saying that "*the opposite of addiction is connection,*" a theme he explores in his book, *Lost Connections: Uncovering the Real Causes of Depression—and the Unexpected Solutions*.[6] This book resonated strongly with me as the issues raised were similar to those identified by Viktor Frankl almost a hundred years ago. Johann's extensive research found nine factors contributing to depression, and seven of the nine related to the way we live, or as

Frankl called it, our "mechanistic" lives.

We are relational beings who have turned over our communal responsibilities to transactional systems that have disconnected us from ourselves, each other, and the natural world. "*Just like bees evolved to need a hive, humans evolved to need a tribe,*" says Johann. He summarized his findings as follows:

> *The more I investigated depression and anxiety, the more I found that, far from being caused by a spontaneously malfunctioning brain, depression and anxiety are mostly being caused by events in our lives. If you find your work meaningless and you feel you have no control over it, you are far more likely to become depressed. If you are lonely and feel that you can't rely on the people around you to support you, you are far more likely to become depressed. If you think life is all about buying things and climbing up the ladder, you are far more likely to become depressed. If you think your future will be insecure, you are far more likely to become depressed. I started to find a whole blast of scientific evidence that depression and anxiety are not caused in our skulls, but by the way many of us are being made to live. There are real biological factors, like your genes, that can make you significantly more sensitive to these causes, but they are not the primary drivers.*[7]

I began to follow Johann on social media channels and learned about Patreon, a platform that allows people to support writers, artists, and more to do their work. On Johann's Patreon page, monthly contributions of $2 to $250 allow him to travel and do the deep research needed to create his thought-provoking books. I immediately became a Patreon supporter. I widely share his books and TED Talks (especially, "This Could Be Why You Are Depressed or Anxious"[8]) as I think they provide well-researched perspectives and highlight inspiring people contributing to change in their communities.

Johann's most recent book, *Stolen Focus: Why You Can't Pay Attention—And How to Think Deeply Again*, became one of the bestselling books of 2022. It provides a brilliant look at the wide variety of social, environmental, nutritional, and institutional factors affecting our lives. While we often blame technology, particularly social

145

media, as a primary cause of our societal ills, he shows a broader view of the multi-layered unhealthy ecosystem that affects our lives. From unhealthy chemicals in our food and air to our dysfunctional addiction to growth, Johann challenges us to look at the impact on our planet and the plants, animals, and people who depend on its vitality.

There was one story in *Stolen Focus* that emotionally affected me. It was about cribbing, which is when horses nervously chew on the sides of their stall. This does not happen in nature; it is caused by the stress of confinement. This confinement and separation from the natural world are distressing to all living organisms, including humans. We are designed to engage with others and the natural environment, yet we live in closed systems. I see this distress exhibited by children who are confined to classrooms and school buildings for hours on end. We label and medicate them to tolerate the stress. How can we, as parents, change this for our children? How can we become good ancestors to future generations?

DR. AI ADDYSON-ZHANG

Working on my blog led me to LinkedIn, and one of my earliest connections was with Dr. Ai Addyson-Zhang, who left her tenured university position to build a new type of school, *Classroom Without Walls*.[9] She also hosted a podcast called *What Is School For: Discuss, Debate, and Disrupt Education* and invited me to be a guest after reading my blog. I learned about her personal story growing up in China and, although it is a different country, its themes of ranking, shaming, and competition reminded me of some of the reasons we are seeing all too common "abnormal reactions" like anxiety, depression, addiction, and suicide in our U.S. youth.

The now vibrant and energetic professor describes the academic climate of her childhood and teen years in China as a time of despair. Her school life was extremely isolating, as her teachers continually reminded the class that everyone around them was a competitor, not a friend. Testing was routine, and after every test, the scores were placed on the board next to the students' names. They would then take a seat in the classroom—front to back—depending on their test scores. Furthering the humiliation, parents had to attend regular meetings and were required to sit in their child's seat. Thus, the performance of the student reflected on the status of the family and increased academic pressure at home. Ai suffered chronic anxiety, developed an eating disorder, and contemplated suicide.

Given the circumstances, Ai's reaction seems normal and understandable. While it's not as blatant in the U.S., we do follow the same protocols here, with class rankings, award assemblies, and standardized testing. Students compete against each other for grades, test scores, and extracurricular recognition. College admittance is a status symbol for families, and the pressure to build an academic and extracurricular résumé is paramount in many homes. The "front seat" students get admitted to the most prestigious universities, while the rest are left to feel ashamed. As a society, we give little value to nonacademic interests or alternative pathways. Ironically, these alternatives—ranging from trades to caregiving—are the backbone that allow our society to function.

Ai emigrated to the U.S. and continued her education through to a Ph.D. She taught social media at a large public university for ten years. She was continually dismayed to see the distress in her students, who were more focused on grades and test scores than learning the material she was teaching them. She would work hard to bring guest speakers into the classroom to talk about what they were doing, but students were more interested in knowing whether they would get credit for attending. When she expressed concerns to fellow professors, she was shunned. She left the university with the dream of starting a new type of school.

Although Ai had no entrepreneurial experience, she forged ahead.

She developed *Classroom Without Walls* and started her podcast. One of the most impactful thought leaders she had on her show was Seth Godin. He could tell by her questioning that she was looking for a roadmap to success and advised her that the only way to figure it out was to do it. He went on to tell her not to be afraid to fail because failure is the way to learn.

Today, while raising three sons, Ai has evolved into becoming a career and life coach for teenagers and young adults. She has been featured in *Glamour*, *Forbes*, Katie Couric Media, Inside Higher Education, the Today Show, and others. From her work with students all over the world to the hundreds of podcast guests she has hosted to her classroom experience, Ai sees a lack of confidence and motivation in young people. She says that they are struggling to figure out who they are and what direction to go in. This paralysis is not unanticipated in a society that has kept them confined. How do they gain the confidence to figure things out on their own when they can't challenge the narratives they are taught?

PETER HOSTRAWSER

I heard Peter Hostrawser[10] on Ai's podcast and was so impressed to see a teacher with a clear understanding of the challenges facing his profession. Despite constant bureaucratic roadblocks that at times make him question staying, Peter continues to do his best to advocate for students within the system. He teaches business, entrepreneurship, and real-life skills at a public high school outside of Chicago. His tagline is, *"My value is to help you show your value."*

Peter's father was a high school teacher who advised his son not to go into the teaching profession. However, his own difficult experiences *"going through the system"* inspired him to get involved. He started the podcast *Disrupt Education*, highlighting journeys outside the traditional education system and showcasing educational reformers. The podcast keeps him grounded in real-world skills and opportunities for change.

Peter periodically writes blog posts about his experiences as a teacher, and one in particular, "Great Teachers Are NOT Superheroes," offers an inspiring look at his commitment. His students were challenged to help the school district figure out better communication methods to reach parents and other stakeholders. Here is how Peter describes the night before their presentation:

> *School and district administrators will be here tomorrow to view the pitches for improvement . . . and I'm very nervous. Even though each team has practiced their pitches several times, I still see a lot of students sleeping on this project. Well, it looks like they are. Time will tell.*
>
> *I have to get out of their way and help them understand their teams will have to experience this tomorrow no matter what. I have seen greatness and awfulness in their pitches. I want to help every step of the way. My bosses will be in the room tomorrow. I am afraid of looking like a "bad teacher." I am afraid for the kids to look bad in front of professionals.*
>
> *Unlike a superhero . . . I won't swoop in to save them.*
>
> *You see, great teachers will help our students fail. That's right . . . fail. There is learning through failure. So after tomorrow, we will review and assess what happened. Students will have a chance to evaluate their efforts and results. They will be in a safe place to learn entrepreneurship. Because we all know the world is a harsh place.*
>
> *Even though I want to help them like a superhero . . . I have to let them learn through experience. I have given them guidance and help along the way, and ultimately, they will need to take that and build on their own.*
>
> *It's terrifying as a teacher sometimes. . . . In order for our students to learn something, they will need to be tested by doing . . . without bubbling in answers. And that's how we all learn best.[11]*

When I spoke to Peter about this experience, he said it was nerve-wracking, though the students' ideas were ultimately well received. He said, "*It was a risk because I do not have tenure, but I knew it was the right thing to do.*" I asked him what gives him the hope he needs to carry on. He told me that he changed schools a couple of years ago, and the culture shift has been a huge relief. He feels supported by his administration and the superintendent. Most of all, he knows the contribution he makes affects the lives of his students.

ZIZ ABDUR-RA'OOF

Ziz Abdur-Ra'oof[12] and I began a correspondence on LinkedIn about our mutual concern for student well-being. Ziz is a former NFL player who has coached and mentored youth throughout his career, working with middle, high school, and college students. He is the author of *Accelerate: A Guided Playbook for Young Dreamers, Scholars, Artists, and Athletes* and an executive coach. In our discussions, Ziz and I kept coming back to the disconnect between real life in our transforming economy and the rigid structure of our education system. As mentors and parents of young adults ourselves, we were seeing this disconnect firsthand.

Soon after the COVID-19 pandemic started and lockdowns were in place, Ziz called me to suggest we start a podcast and share our conversations with a wider audience. We called it *Q-ED Up with Ziz & Pam* and our focus was on discussing the question, *"What does it mean to be educated in the twenty-first century?"*

We only did the podcast for a short time, twenty-three episodes, before the world opened up and other projects demanded our time, but it was a really enjoyable experience. Ziz's career in the sports world and working within schools provided valuable perspective, as did his views as a person of color. It was fun to explore different subjects and share connections. Both of us advocate for the valuable role of mentorship and the importance of meaning in the lives of students. There were no conclusions reached or directives given, just an offering of possible ways to shift our current paradigm. As this showed, contributions can come from openly discussing different viewpoints and challenging current narratives.

TIM SALAU

When I saw the tagline "Mr. Future of Work" and read his posts, I knew Tim Salau[13] was going to be an inspiring person. His energetic approach to reimagining the future of work, living, and learning aligned with my own human-centered perspective. His experiences coming from Nigeria to a poor Texas community and going through the education system to get multiple college degrees shaped his life purpose. The bullying and hardship he endured fuel his focus on strengthening the bonds people share through empathic and compassionate action.

At the time we connected, Tim was just striking out on his own to co-found Guide, a global lifestyle brand with the mission of equipping every creator with the skills, mindset, and opportunities for a fulfilling career. Guide is a SaaS platform he created after years of working for tech giants such as Google, Microsoft, Facebook, and WeWork. Guide started as a mentor and mentee program, and I signed up. Tim and I have stayed in touch ever since. With our common mission, we share ideas and challenge each other about our different approaches and perspectives.

Tim describes himself as a purpose-driven leader who champions company culture and innovation through community building. He has a special place in his heart for making the world more inclusive for underprivileged leaders, women, LGBTQ+, and people who come from underserved communities.

Every time I talk with Tim, he tells me about a new venture he is embarking upon. He has mastered the art of the pivot. He's an artist, author, keynote speaker, tech influencer, and *"the only Nigerian–African American activist leading and shaping the discussion on the future of work, education, leadership, and innovation."* Most recently, he received his doctorate in psychology and has begun to practice.

Tim exemplifies the many arenas we all can play in to create a life of meaning and purpose. The biggest lesson he's learned in life is that "*the only constant is change, and adaptability, resilience, and innate curiosity are the most essential skills of the twenty-first century.*"

A standardized curriculum could not prepare Tim for the life he is leading. He has learned to trust himself, follow his intuitive conscience, and focus on his contributions to improving the lives of others. Tim shared with me his parents' concern when he told them he was leaving his full-time job to strike out on his own. I think this is always in the back of every parent's mind. We want our children to be safe and secure, and we perceive that full-time work is the way to achieve that. However, in reality, "security" is an illusion, and our adherence to it comes at a high price. As discussed earlier, when we can't become our authentic selves, it can lead to a void in us that gets filled with aggression, addiction, and depression.

DR. SUNIYA LUTHAR

While writing my blog, I often quoted well-respected sources. One of these sources, researcher and clinical psychologist Suniya Luthar,[14] became a friend and collaborator. While pursuing her doctorate in developmental psychology at Yale, Suniya studied inner-city adolescents. She came across an interesting finding that "*kids who were popular were also quite badly behaved, disruptive in class, and so on.*" The question in her mind was, "*Is this an adolescent phenomenon or an inner-city phenomenon?*" She decided to compare these adolescents to those living in suburban areas near the Yale community and found that the suburban kids performed worse than the inner-city kids "*on every index of substance abuse, substance use, cigarettes, alcohol, hard drugs—all of these.*"

Suniya remembers, "*The suburban kids were doing more poorly with depression and anxiety. They were higher than norms on rates of significant problems. This came as a complete surprise to me. I kept thinking, 'There's got to be some mistakes somewhere.'"* However, multiple part data points highlighted the same conclusion. Today, students at public and private high-achieving schools (those with high standardized test scores and graduates going to top colleges) are considered "at risk," along with those who have been exposed to poverty, trauma, and discrimination.

Suniya has led multi-year longitudinal studies seeking to understand these problems and where they come from. She says it is incredibly naive to say that *"if you've got a college degree and you've got a six-figure salary, then you should be fine."* Her research found that there are different sets of stresses. *"The inner-city mom is worried about her child out at dusk and needs to keep a child off the streets away from gang members or those who recruit."* In the case of the more affluent mom, there is the mentality that *"if you can do more, you must do more with no sense of, or little sense of when it's time to say, 'this is not healthy and we need to stop.' So the risks are different, but they're in some ways equally powerful and in some ways, more so."*

"One of the most fascinating things, parenthetically, I remember is when you looked at children of depressed moms as compared to children of substance abusing moms, it was actually the former that were more vulnerable." She sums it up this way: *"When a child is in pain, or for that matter, an adult is in pain, it doesn't matter what their street address is."*

In 2016, Suniya published an article called "Who Mothers Mommy?"[15] **Her research showed that emotional resilience in children was strongly associated with the health and well-being of their primary caregiver, usually their mother.** She found that the main factors that decrease stress for mothers were unconditional acceptance, authentic personal relationships, and the feeling of emotional comfort. In other words, mothers need to be cared for as much as their children do. Human beings need to be connected to one another; it is how we have survived throughout our evolution.

If we as a society want our children to do well, we must ensure that the primary caregiver or caregivers are doing well. As Suniya says, "*We need to care for the caregivers.*" This applies to educators and medical professionals as well. "*Without support, those suffering from burnout—which is a high percentage today—are unable to give their full attention to the needs of children in their care.*"

Suniya went on to develop a twelve-week small group program that fosters support for authentic connections. In 2019, it was peer-reviewed and published by the National Academies of Sciences, Engineering, and Medicine as an effective, low-cost model. Continued support after the groups are completed is essential to ongoing health and well-being, which is why one of the first things that these groups teach participants is to create a broader community-based network of support outside the group.

When Suniya talked to me about offering her program to mothers, educators, medical professionals, and others through a nonprofit called AC Groups, I provided the necessary financial support. I now serve on the board and steering committee to spread the valuable and compassionate lifelines these groups help create.

Unfortunately, I can't write about all the people I have connected with and admire. I suggest you check out some of my other LinkedIn friends who are doing their part to contribute to change for our children, including Matt Barnes (Parent Whisperer and Founder of The Education Game), Blake Boles (Director of Unschool Adventures and author of *Why Are You Still Sending Your Kids to School? The Case for Helping Them Leave, Chart Their Own Paths, and Prepare for Adulthood at Their Own Pace*), Kevin J. Fleming. Ph.D. (Founder and CEO of Catapult), Dagmar Kauffmann (Founder of On Balance Parenting), and Mike Yates (Senior Production Manager of Reinvention Lab at Teach for America and podcast host of *Schoolish*).

ORGANIZATIONS BUILDING INFRASTRUCTURE

In addition to individuals, there are organizations playing a role in the shift we are now seeing in education and creating new infrastructure to support the change. One of my favorites is Education Reimagined, founded by Kelly Young, which is a nonprofit working to bring to life a new vision for public education. It connects and mobilizes education changemakers and galvanizes resources to create and demonstrate possibilities. In 2022, they introduced The Big Idea[16] to demonstrate and inspire the development of community-based learning ecosystems, showing what a new public education system could look like and how it would work. It recognizes that *"learning lives everywhere—at recreation centers, parks, public libraries, museums, office buildings, colleges, community gardens, theaters, churches, homes, and in backyards."* The model is closely aligned with what we are doing at B-Unbound.

I originally met Carlos, Co-Executive Director of Big Picture Learning, through one of Education Reimagined's informative webinars and connected with Kelly to get her thoughts about our education film. I have since written articles for their newsletter, *Voyager*. Elliot and I visited Kelly in Washington, D.C., in 2021 to discuss our mutual missions. During the meeting, Kelly described her frustration as a parent trying to support her young teenage son, Tucker, in pursuing his obsession with cars. Opportunities seemed too far away or inappropriate for his age or specific interest. Elliot suggested she talk with Big Picture Learning's Charlie Plant. In a *Voyager* newsletter article she shared Charlie's advice and how she turned it into action:

> *Charlie immediately said, "You don't have to travel far to find someone who is noodling with a car. The world is full of tinkerers. They are all around us and would love to talk to a young person like your son." His advice was so simple. The key, he said, is that Tucker, or any young person, find a community of people practicing a craft who will take an interest in him and support him to develop his skills such that he is respected by that community in that craft. It doesn't matter*

what the skill is. It is the process itself—of seeking out a space to grow, develop, and find belonging—that will be replicable all through his life.[17]

Kelly went on to describe how she pulled into a gas station to fill her car up and, on a whim, asked the owner if he had any internship opportunities. He said that he used to have four high schoolers every summer working at the station, but no one had applied in thirteen years. Her son met with the owner the next day and ended up with a paid job. With Charlie as an advisor, Kelly played the role of Co-Navigator for her son. Every parent can do this.

VELA Education Fund[18] is a national nonprofit organization launched in 2019 to support the creation and amplification of community-based contributions. As their website says:

> *VELA invests in everyday entrepreneurs—students, parents, educators, and community leaders—who are envisioning new approaches that meet learners' and families' needs. These models include homeschool co-ops, microschools, after-school programs, and much, much more. VELA does not dictate solutions to its grantees. Instead, VELA trusts grantees to identify what their communities need and how they can best meet those needs.*

The support for educational change is very much needed. I have been inspired by the number of people and organizations focused on solutions rather than arguing about the problem of a broken system. Other organizations actively working to honor individual contributions include:

Praxis, a college alternative that offers a year-long program matching students to a full-time paid apprenticeship.

Populace, a think-tank started by Todd Rose. They are working to shift our cultural narrative around success and advocating for the transformation of systems to better meet the personal needs of individuals and communities.

Tear the Paper Ceiling, a nonprofit coalition led by Opportunity@ Work and AD Council that partners with companies to break down the barriers facing "*STARs—workers who are Skilled Through Alternative Routes, rather than through a Bachelor's Degree.*"

EVERY ACTION MATTERS

These contributions are creating waves of change. There are too many to name in this book—and that's a good thing, because the cultural shift we need will not come from a single source. It must come from all of us contributing who we are, from where we are, for the betterment of our communities and the society in which our children are raised.

Every action matters. What we decide to do today shapes our tomorrow. Together, we are co-creating our world. If we want a world that recognizes the value and dignity of each individual and their important contribution to the whole, then we must work together. Be a ripple in the wave of change.

Our competitive judging of individual achievement has not led to a healthy society. Look around at the overwhelming emotional, physical, and financial distress we have created. We are raising our children in this environment. We train them to focus on what they can get for themselves rather than seeing that they are part of something bigger and have an important contribution to make based on who they are as individuals. The denial of their unique individuality in servitude to the community is not the answer. The answer lies in their responsibility to a greater whole and their freely chosen decision of how best to contribute.

In order for our children to learn how to face life's challenges, we need to model for them. In all our fallible humanness, we are each uniquely called to answer the demands placed on us by life. There are so many ways to participate in creating communities that promote human flourishing. It could be a grandmother deciding to sit on a bench and listen to someone's story or even watching children play in the park while parents are working. It could be a parent shifting priorities so their children have time to nurture relationships and explore their curiosities and interests. It could be someone taking the time to share their interest or skill with a young person. Each will be specific to the individual and cannot be decided for them. The main goal is to expand possibilities for interconnectedness and contribution in our communities. These demands are specific to us individually and relate to the circumstances we find ourselves in. The best part is that this could help us discover meaning and purpose in our own lives.

———

CHAPTER 8

IF NOT NOW, WHEN?

Yesterday is gone. Tomorrow has not yet come. You have only today.
Let us begin.

—Mother Teresa

I spent the first half of my life waiting for my real life to start. I had been taught and believed that I needed to complete my education and establish my career before settling down and having the family I desired. I achieved the success markers defined by our culture: college degree, good salary, management position. I raced to each goalpost as fast as I could, the blinders I wore keeping me focused on the next thing and the next. But as I approached my mid-30s and my workload and travel schedule consumed my days, I hit an emotional and physical wall.

The achievements and accolades felt empty. The never-ending tasks—reports, meetings, presentations—felt like a treadmill of busyness with no end in sight. I had always loved children, and between my business trips, I began volunteering at a public school and a homeless daycare center. I dreamed of having my own children someday, but someday never seemed to materialize.

Unexplainable stomachaches and a sudden fear of flying stopped me in my tracks. Although uncomfortable at the time, they gave me the gift of reflection. I realized that I had not created space in my life for the things that really mattered to me; I assumed they would just happen without much effort. This time of reflection motivated me to make a radical decision, and I resigned from my well-paying job so I could refocus my life to align with my values.

I remember waking up one night in terror at what I had done. *I have a mortgage and a car payment. What am I going to do?* But when these thoughts came in, I sent them out again. I intuitively understood, in the depths of my being, that I couldn't continue as I had been and had to trust that I could handle whatever came my way. I firmly believe that when we align ourselves with our intuitive knowing, the road will rise to meet us. It did for me.

I cared a lot about the people I worked with and felt a responsibility to ensure the transition was as smooth as possible. I gave three months' notice, found a replacement to run the office, and started talking with people in my field to figure out where my lifestyle choices and skills could fit. I soon became a consultant working independently, and my finances remained steady. Without meetings, quarterly reporting, and all the other bureaucratic responsibilities, I could do my work in less time. This freed up my schedule to devote time to dating, and within a few years, I was married, and my children were born.

Stepping off that treadmill and into life was the best decision I ever made. I look upon my three daughters with tremendous joy and gratitude. Based on my experience of waiting for life to start, I fiercely guarded their childhoods so they could play, explore, and spend time with their grandparents and friends. I was unwilling to trade the present moment for the demands of academic achievement or the promise of some future financial gain. I admit that the cultural tide was strong, and I often felt like a salmon swimming upstream—but it was so worth it.

The price we are paying to prepare our children for our societal definition of success is high, and the toll on mental health and wellness is heartbreaking. Relationships have become transactional rather than nurturing, with interactions centered around lists of tasks and calendar events. We reinforce the dictates of schools and organizations in our homes, even though they overwhelm and exhaust us. We sacrifice our family time and our children's unique interests to ensure tasks are completed so grades across all subjects are high. We are shocked by how fast time passes and regret how we ignored so many opportunities to enjoy life.

The way we live our lives is teaching our children that being productive and efficient are the most important values, that life is linear rather than constantly twisting and turning, and that other people know what is best for them. We reinforce the idea that their actions will be responded to in an organized, timely manner with a grade, test score, or verbal feedback, instead of teaching them the skill of self-assessment.

Self-assessment requires paying attention to intuition and the signs and signals of life to make decisions. This type of assessment will carry our children throughout their lives. Their familiarity with controlled feedback loops, not readily available in the messiness of the real world, makes the transition to adulthood difficult for many students.

WAITING FOR WHEN

We rush through our day-to-day lives, preparing our children for someday when they will arrive at a point where they have enough financial security to avoid life's suffering. With all eyes looking far ahead, our children learn that life is about waiting for when. When you graduate high school, when you get to college, when you get a job. We keep them focused on the future. It is a cultural obsession.

But this orientation creates disembodiment. We leave the present moment and live in an imaginary future, and because the future is unknown and uncertain, this disembodiment causes a great deal of anxiety—for us and our children. While stressful periods happen, this future-focused obsession makes it never-ending. It is hard to enjoy life when concern about the unknown consumes our daily existence.

In 1951, Alan Watts wrote *The Wisdom of Insecurity: A Message for an Age of Anxiety*. Sadly, the title still applies to our world today because it relates to the materialistic and mechanistic way of life we have adopted. He noted that directing actions toward future pleasures takes away the enjoyment of the present, and only complete awareness of the present *"could even begin to guarantee future happiness."*

Life only happens in the present moment. Meaning is found moment to moment, situation by situation, and person by person. Each one of us can co-create our life using our innate gifts and what we can contribute to our current circumstances. The decisions we make in all these moments make our lives meaningful and define who we are. Responding to life as it unfolds and relying on our conscience to guide us can help alleviate some of the worry and stress of uncertainty.

So much of life cannot be planned. It just happens, and if we have blinders on, we may miss opportunities. Vocational psychologist John Krumboltz's theory of "planned happenstance" says that indecision is a normal response to an uncertain future. He advised his clients to get out into the world, do things, and meet people. In this way, "happenstance" or unexpected opportunities can come about if they are open to seeing them.[1]

Imagine if our children learned to be open, to explore things that interested them, and to find people who could support them along the way. Imagine the aliveness they would feel from the adventure into uncertainty when *they* are in the driver's seat. Freed from the constraints of our past perspectives, what contributions could they make to our world?

Waiting for when leads to a life of passive existence. The safety and security promised to our children if they follow a prescribed path is an illusion and limits human potential. It has also proven to be a financial disaster for many students and their families, not to mention the toll it has taken on our collective mental health. The silver lining to the COVID-19 pandemic is that more of us are waking up to the realization that we no longer want to be disembodied; we want to be whole and human. The possibilities are endless if we live in the present, recognize the valuable contributions of each and every person, and support our children in navigating their own way.

FIGURING IT OUT

Opening the gates and freeing our children is easier said than done. They are so used to confinement that the freedom to choose can be difficult. It reminds me of baby elephants who have a rope tied around their ankle when they are young. As they grow and get more powerful, the rope turns into a chain that they could easily break, but they are so used to the limitation that they don't question it. Their power is constrained by their thinking and conditioning.

Our societal dictates have conditioned our children to suppress their individuality and decision-making abilities. They have become fragile within the confines of structures that have kept them on a narrow pathway to our society's definition of success.

Within my family and community, I have seen young people refuse to continue waiting for life to begin. My nephews, Ryan and Corey, had no interest in going to college after they graduated high school twenty years ago. They wanted to enter the workforce. At the time, we were all horrified. How would they succeed in life without a college degree? They were varsity athletes, financially able to attend college, and one even had a scholarship. But they could not be dissuaded, and to their credit, their parents honored their choices.

They went to work for companies where they started in entry-level positions: one in a warehouse and one as a truck driver. Through their hard work and dedication, as well as in-house training, they rose to become managers. They are now in their 30s and earn more than most college graduates their age (both earn six figures), with the added advantage of not having student loan debt. They own homes, have families, and can make advancement choices based on their values, not financial necessity.

I see many of the youth in my community, and specifically those I mentor, struggling to reconcile the life they were promised after they checked all the boxes with the life they find once they are out in the real world. James[2] is a young adult in his mid-20s who followed the prescribed pathway to college and the workforce. He is an avid learner but not academically inclined, so the road to and through college was not an easy one for him. After he graduated, he found himself in a cubicle, selling things to people that he wasn't sure they needed, but he received a nice paycheck every two weeks. His parents were proud, and his community could point to his success, but he wasn't living as his authentic self.

James is a person who loves the outdoors, cares about community, and enjoys making things. After a couple of years, he couldn't sit in the cubicle anymore, and so he quit. He began exploring work in the hospitality field that related to his love of hiking and surfing. He moved in and out of various jobs, mostly for small companies, but still couldn't land on the exact thing he wanted to do. During this time, the malaise he previously felt about his life disappeared. It was a struggle, yes, but he owned the journey.

After a couple of more years, he was tired of bouncing around and wanted a secure job with a regular paycheck. His experiences qualified him for a well-paying assistant manager position at a large hotel that was part of a prestigious chain. He entered the company during the COVID-19 pandemic, when turnover in the hospitality industry was extremely high. The company culture was tense, with customers frustrated by the lack of staff and constant turnover, which was exhausting for those who stayed. As with most large corporations, the focus was on spreadsheets and revenue, not people.

After several months, James had no quality of life, was working all the time, and his social life was suffering. He spoke to his manager, and they offered him a management position in the fitness and spa department for even more money. He was 26 years old and had been there less than a year. The new position was slightly better, but the company culture remained unchanged. After working for the company for a year and a half, James quit. He will no longer trade his life for the bottom line of a balance sheet.

We must realize that making a living is one component of our life, but it can affect many other areas that impact our mental and physical well-being. If we are exhausted and drained by our workday, our relationships, self-care, and meaningful endeavors can suffer. The pandemic sparked a reevaluation for millions. Many well-paying corporate jobs are unfilled. Some of this is due to a lack of skills, but some of it relates to personal choices about how people want to live. And people want to *live*.

The work in our digital and industrial organizations can be unfulfilling at any price, and some of the cultures are toxic to well-being, as James experienced. In our current economy, human beings have often become a means to an end for organizations to achieve their goals, but a cultural shift is taking place. Meaning and purpose have risen to become highly valued and an important consideration in the work many young people choose to do. They are in the driver's seat and deciding to create a different way of living.

ENGAGEMENT OVER PRODUCTIVITY

What would our society look like if we prioritized **engagement over productivity**? We have become so focused on production that we have lost sight of the most important parts of being human. What if the meaningful contributions and relationships of individuals were viewed as valuable to the whole? What if teachers could spend time developing relationships with their students or doctors could spend time getting to know their patients? While we can mass-produce inanimate objects like pencils, the same principles cannot be applied to living organisms, especially human beings. It reduces them to a single variable and ignores the life force provided by ecosystems that we don't fully see or understand.

I had lunch recently with a very successful businessman who was lamenting about structural unemployment and how terrible it is for the economy. I view it differently. To me, the industrialized structure that is based on consumerism has been devastating to humanity. It is inequitable, uses too much of the earth's resources, and devalues living organisms.

As the old structure begins to disintegrate, a new paradigm is being built. We don't yet have ways to measure it, but in addition to the traditional full-time economy, I see it in the new work-from-home economy, freelance economy, and sharing economy. I see it in communities coming together to share and trade. I see it in the type of skill-specific, project-oriented work and the new short-term training programs now available that are creating new options. I see it in the new lifestyle choices being made based on values and the communication channels developed to facilitate in-person connection.

The changing nature of the economy is creating freedom in lifestyle choices that accommodate caregiving and personal interests, as well as the ability to pursue more meaningful work. The potential of earning a college degree is available to all ages at any point in life and from almost any location. Even shortened competency-based programs are being introduced at popular institutions like Western Governors University and Southern New Hampshire University.

Even more importantly, there are now many avenues for gaining needed skills that don't require a college degree. For example, companies are increasingly developing their own programs. The apprenticeship model is expanding beyond the trades, and short-term credentialing services are now available. There are trade and technical skills certifications offered, both online and in-person, through some college extension programs and private enterprises. These areas are rapidly growing.

There is no certainty in the future, and it is our fear of uncertainty that keeps us stuck. Years ago, I was reading an article written by a futurist who gave this advice to parents: "*Embrace uncertainty.*" What happens when we stop producing for the sake of production and start engaging with life—other people, nature, and ideas? Could this make life less lonely? Could we begin to see how our individual uniqueness is valuable to our communities? Could we come to know that a meaningful life comes from what we share of ourselves, not what we get?

WAITING ON INSTITUTIONAL CHANGE

We have become a society that waits. We wait for institutions to change, or we wait for the right politician to get elected. But in reality, these are laggers of change, not initiators. True societal shifts happen organically from the bottom up, not the top down. The entrenched frameworks of our industrial-model institutions—with their financial entanglements—make high-level change difficult at best and extremely slow. We cannot wait. **Each one of us must contribute today—small or large—to change the unhealthy environments in which we are raising our children.** Our decisions today change our tomorrows.

As a parent, I need to encourage my children to take responsibility for driving themselves on their journey through life. I have to step back and let them explore, even if it is not always successful. Guided by their conscience, they need to make decisions specific to their unique individuality, interests, and goals. They need to understand that they have a responsibility to share their uniqueness for the betterment of the world, whether that is in giving to other people or causes they care about.

This idea of sharing themselves for the benefit of something greater is a shift from how we have raised children in our modern society. We have taught them to value themselves by what they get—a grade, test score, money, win, likes, and followers—not what they give. And what they give has to be their decision or it leads to burnout and resentment. The collective cannot tell them what they need to contribute. It is a delicate balance between individuality and community.

The world they are entering is not the one we are familiar with, so allowing them agency is essential. The toughest thing is letting go of the expectation that they need to follow a path that may have "worked" for us or that our vision of success fits with theirs. They are the ones who must own their choices and the consequences. Having them rely on us or other authority figures to tell them what they should do is not a long-term strategy for raising resilient, fulfilled human beings.

THE WILD, WILD WEST

A new frontier has opened, and opportunities abound. Rather than moving across a physical landscape with covered wagons, this frontier moves across time and space, enabled by technology. New virtual communities made up of people with similar beliefs, interests, training, and work have sprung up seemingly overnight. Whereas we were once limited by geography, this new frontier allows us to connect with people all over the world, exchanging ideas, money, goods, and services.

The similarities between this virtual world and the physical one where pioneers moved west are uncanny. In addition to spreading out and establishing new communities, there has been the creation of robber barons (or if you prefer, captains of industry), those few men who garnered most of the wealth by creating new industries. In place of J.P. Morgan, Carnegie, Rockefeller, and Mellon, we now have Gates, Jobs, Zuckerberg, and Bezos. And there is even a gold rush, as the cryptocurrencies of today have obsessive followings and rampant speculation, similar to the gold nuggets frantically mined by the forty-niners.

The seismic economic shift that is occurring is akin to the Industrial Revolution, only it is bigger because it is faster moving and global. It affects every aspect of our lives and is changing how we relate to one another. Who could conceive that we would spend billions of dollars to ride in a stranger's car (Uber) or sleep in a stranger's bed (Airbnb)? Who could have seen that seemingly solid corporate structures would dissolve and new forms of person-to-person commerce would emerge?

The next stage of this shift will be in combining the resources of the virtual world and physical spaces to enable important human-to-human connections. Our physical proximity to others matters. Peer support can enhance learning. This is not to say that everyone must do school or work in a physical location, but their lives must somehow be anchored in a physical community of belonging to avoid isolation.

How do we prepare our children for this new frontier? One thing is for sure: the overwhelming amount of content and the hours devoted to memorization, homework, and organized activities are restricting their ability to develop the skill sets needed to navigate this societal and economic transformation. It is their antifragility—their ability to face challenges head-on—that will support their pioneering in this new era. **Knowledge will not give our children wisdom; experience is what will give them wisdom.**

THE ONLY WAY FORWARD IS THROUGH

The Wizard of Oz provides a narrative road map for navigating uncertain times. Our houses have crashed down into a new land (a new era). We can only go forward. With technological changes driving rapid transformation in all areas of our lives and an awakening to the harmful effects of the way we live, many of us are seeing that we are "not in Kansas anymore."

The story serves as an illustration of our societal beliefs. The Wizard reminds me of our unwavering belief that someone else knows best for us. We believe college will bestow worthiness, wealth, and status upon our children if we can get them there, just like Dorothy believes that the Wizard holds the power to get her home if she can get to the Emerald City.

Dorothy is told to follow the yellow brick road and it will lead her to where she needs to go, just as we tell our children that they must all follow the same path through our education systems. Dorothy's long road through Oz is fraught with pitfalls, sickness, and fear, as is our children's long road to building the necessary résumé for college admissions. Dorothy is constantly competing against the Wicked Witch of the West, and our children are constantly competing against our societal expectations that seek to define who they are and what they should become.

But the hidden message in the story highlights the way forward: along the yellow brick road, Dorothy meets the Tin Man, Cowardly Lion, and Scarecrow. Each is insecure, believing that they are inadequate in some way, but they transcend themselves to save each other. They each contribute who they uniquely are to the situation at hand, and their collective contributions change their circumstances. Together, they figure out how to meet the demands of the moment.

Each one of the characters is irreplaceable and plays a critical role in accomplishing their mission. Not one offers the same perspective or can make the same type of contribution. The gift each of them is called to share challenges their perceived inadequacies.

The Tin Man is sad because he is hollow and doesn't have a heart. He causes himself to rust when he cries, "*If I only had a heart!*" But his compassion and care for his companions along the journey show that he can love and be loved. It doesn't matter that he was made differently.

The Cowardly Lion is afraid even though his species is supposed to be fearless. He frequently exclaims, "*If I only had the courage!*" He learns that he can overcome his fear when he cares more about Dorothy and his companions than himself. His love helps him gain courage over his fears and brings meaning and purpose to his life.

The Scarecrow doesn't believe he is smart because he doesn't have a piece of paper that tells him he is smart. He laments, "*If I only had a brain!*" throughout the story. Yet, he masterminds the journey to the Wicked Witch's castle and rescues Dorothy, proving he already had a brain, and the degree wasn't necessary to prove it.

Dorothy is lost and afraid but determined that the Wizard will save her. She follows what others tell her to do rather than being responsible for herself. But in the end, she has no choice but to save herself and throws water on the Wicked Witch. She uses adaptability, creativity, empathy, and collaboration to help guide her through the upheaval she experiences. These were human qualities she already possessed.

Once the curtain is pulled back by her small dog, she realizes that the Wizard was not the all-powerful savior she wanted him to be. She comes to understand that the power was inside her all along. She needs only to recognize her responsibility and decision-making abilities, and then she clicks her ruby-red shoes and returns to her family and community.

Throughout the story, we see the power of collective effort to achieve desired outcomes and the importance of following intuitive knowledge. In the end, it is the innocent dog, Toto, who pulls the curtain back and exposes the truth. **Our children have pulled the curtain back and exposed the high price of societal expectations. Are we paying attention?**

Freeing our children to learn to authentically navigate themselves through different stages of life—well beyond the time they live with us—necessitates that they know how to listen to their inner guidance and get connected to others who can support them along the way. Contributing their unique abilities, talents, and perspectives to the situations they find themselves in is essential. To do this, we must redefine our societal expectations and create conditions that expand possibilities for each and every child.

Professor Leo Buscaglia advised, *"Don't spend your precious time asking, 'Why isn't the world a better place?' It will only be time wasted. The question to ask is 'How can I make it better?' To that there is an answer, and it all starts from within you."* We have much to do to improve the society in which we are raising our children, and each one of us can contribute to the tasks needed for change.

———

CHAPTER 9

ARE YOU READY FOR THE RIDE?

When we are no longer able to change a situation, we are challenged to change ourselves.

—Viktor Frankl

The moment my daughter challenged me to look at her, really look at her, marked the beginning of my journey to writing this book. I can't tell parents how to raise their children as each child is unique in mind, body, and spirit, as well as circumstances. My responsibility—and the responsibility of all of us—relates to the contributions we make to the societal norms and values that either nurture or hinder human potential. These values are reflected in how we live our daily lives and in the physical and cultural environments we create.

Social narratives are created by communities adhering to norms and beliefs. The good news is that communities are made up of individuals—you and me. Everything we do matters; our individual contributions, whether in attitude or deed, can reinforce or shift our societal norms and conditions. Our paternalistic approach to children, coupled with the level of responsibility we have turned over to institutional systems to prepare and care for them, has not served our society well. We can decide to change this. It is within our power to transform ourselves, and therefore our society, for the benefit of all children.

The epidemic of mental illness, the "dropout" rate, and inequitable opportunities are not a reflection of the failure of individual students; they are indications of the failure of our education system. This failure is expressed in the dehumanizing way we measure the system's success and the intelligence of our children with grades and standardized test scores. No child can be averaged and compared to another, locally or globally. The basis of our approach is deeply flawed and has affected the self-worth of children for decades.

Why are we trying to create a culture of sameness when diversity provides value and strength? Imagination, creativity, and innovation thrive when we are faced with challenges, not when we are all trained to look at things the same way. Diverse perspectives, intelligences, beliefs, and characteristics are advantages, not disadvantages. To invigorate healthy communities, we must embrace our differences.

What kind of world do we want to live in? Do we want our children to spend their early years continuously preparing for life to begin, or do we want them to live a meaningful life now? Do we want them to grow up in isolated silos segmented by age and function or together in multigenerational environments where they are free to explore who they are and decide what they want to become? Rather than driving our children throughout their lives, we can teach them to drive themselves with us in the passenger seat cheering them on.

The mass production approach to life has wreaked havoc on our communities and our planet. Our addiction to growth at all costs has depleted essential resources, including human vitality and energy. The hierarchical pyramids created by this approach leave a large base unseen and unheard. More importantly, it separates us from the critical interactions that help us to thrive. We need to build interconnected social infrastructure in our communities so we are no longer only situationally connected.

News media and politicians like to promote divisiveness to gain viewers and votes, but the truth is most of us share common concerns and desires. Common unity translates into community. Humankind would have been wiped out of existence if there were more bad people than good. Fred Rogers (aka Mister Rogers) tells the following story:

When I was a boy and I would see scary things in the news, my mother would say to me, "Look for the helpers. You will always find people who are helping." To this day, especially in times of "disaster," I remember my mother's words and I am always comforted by realizing that there are still so many helpers—so many caring people in this world.[1]

If our children are out playing in our neighborhood in view of neighbors we know and trust, we don't worry. Imagine if we could have social trust in our larger communities. Imagine if, when our children ventured out, they trusted themselves to intuitively discern who could be trusted? Social trust is generated by the unique contributions each of us makes to the collective ecosystem. We get to know each other through the sharing of responsibilities, the pursuit of meaningful endeavors, and the solving of mutual concerns.

We are all born with a tremendous responsibility to make the most of the time we have been given. **Who we are matters, what we contribute matters, how we engage with the world matters, and why we are needed matters more than anything.** Our unique puzzle piece plays a vital part in creating the picture of life. Our contributions to the world, based on who we are and who we choose to become in each moment, play an essential role in the collective shaping of our local and global communities.

CONTRIBUTION VERSUS LEADERSHIP

To me, someone who leads is a contributor of a specific ability—but they offer only one slice of the pie. They cannot do it alone, and emphasizing leadership creates an imbalance in responsibility and reinforces a hierarchical structure that devalues individual contributions and discourages possibilities. Everyone has a responsibility to contribute who they are to the world, but how, when, where, and to what extent is their decision.

During the years my daughters were in school, I volunteered in a variety of ways to support their schools and activities. Sometimes I would chair a committee, sometimes I would be a worker bee, and sometimes I couldn't be involved at all. What I contributed depended on my abilities, time availability, priorities, and interests. To create the change we want to see, we as parents need only contribute what we can from where we are at any given moment.

Rather than focusing on how everyone should parent, which is impossible and too microscopic, we need to focus on our individual contributions to shaping the environments and culture in which our children are being raised. To accomplish this, we need to recognize that we only have power over ourselves, not our children and not other people. In reality, while we are the drivers of our own lives, we are always in the passenger seat of everyone else's.

Through our contributions and the changes we make in ourselves, the ripple effect begins, and our environments organically change. We are more alike than different, and a society based on trust and respect rather than paternalism will create vibrant communities that promote human flourishing. When our societal values are redefined, the cultural narrative will shift, and we can choose differently. Do we continue to focus on the perpetual growth of an economic machine, or do we focus on nurturing human beings and the planet we all share?

RUNNING PARALLEL

No one needs to change schools, neighborhoods, or workplaces to begin applying the ideas presented in this book. The changes we need to make are within ourselves and involve our free will and responsibility to contribute to desired change. We will all have differing perspectives, abilities, and priorities that affect how we engage with the people and issues that matter to us.

I am not suggesting a revolution. Revolutions with angry participants railing against each other and blaming the system create unnecessary upheaval. I'm suggesting an evolution—a consciously chosen new way of living. We are already seeing this in action as the role, structure, and authority of schools are being reshaped in many communities as parents and educators push back against the current framework.

Microschools are emerging, and there is tremendous growth in homeschooling, particularly in Black communities.[2] Hybrid in-person and online options are now available at some public schools. We still have to address the way we educate our children through content memorization, compliance, and testing, but it is a start.

Several states have also voted to fund students themselves instead of districts (which is typically the entity getting taxpayer dollars).[3] This could encourage new human-centered learning environments and force public schools to transform to compete. On the other hand, it could result in another money grab for taxpayer dollars. The choices made by the parents in those states will determine whether it becomes beneficial to students or part of the same old system.

The molding and shaping of children to fit into our societal constructs are pervasive approaches that can be found in every type of school—public, charter, private, or homeschool. When evaluating schooling options, the main factors to consider are whether your child can be the driver of their own learning journey and whether they are simultaneously gaining real-world experience. Specifically, parents can ask, *"Does this environment help my child learn to navigate their own way?"* and *"Does it connect them to relationships in the community that can help them explore and deepen their interests while fostering a supportive network of peers and adults outside of school?"*

In many cases, trade-offs will have to be made based on the availability of schools in your area or family considerations. In this case, focusing on the parent suggestions offered in Chapter 4 and looking for after-school options like B-Unbound can help students gain necessary support as they learn to take the wheel of their own lives with caring adults alongside them.

The education landscape is rapidly evolving, and many efforts are being made to shift from school-centered to learner-centered practices. Big Picture Learning has shown that this shift can be successful in public schools regardless of the socio-economic environment. The culture of the school and the trust, dignity, and respect given to students play key roles in that success. Regardless of the school, the responsibility for the health and well-being of our children primarily belongs to parents and communities.

We built large institutional systems to help us with the responsibilities of communal life. We separated the specific aspects of life we wanted to turn over and paid taxes to support them. Education, criminal justice, foster care, agriculture, social services, and other systems emerged out of this desire. But these systems have ended up taking on a life of their own as each person within them is removed from the direct impact of their decisions on people in their community.

Our systems feed other systems, they do not nurture human beings, nor do they promote thriving communities. We have unleashed Frankenstein's monster by turning over the bulk of personal and community responsibility to these systems without paying attention to their massive failure in providing what we hoped. Too many of us have become "lost" in the systems when trying to find help in solving our unique and specific challenges.

I am not suggesting that we do not need these systems. We do. They can help provide supportive safety nets for our communities. If I break my leg, I want to go to the clinic or hospital. However, these systems have been overburdened with frontline responsibility and have been inappropriately given decision-making power for the care of individuals. We lose our agency when we walk through their doors. This is true for education, healthcare, foster care, and all social services.

Sadly, by their design, these systems have also ended up contributing to many of our social ills. They have produced a nation of debtors who rely on these systems. Healthcare and student loan debt, added to other obligatory payments to use the services, have been financially and emotionally crushing to many people. As we recognize this truth, we can move forward to support human values by realigning responsibilities.

ACTIONABLE STEPS

We can all contribute to this realignment of responsibilities. Here are a few ideas to get you started.

At Home

Depending on your home life, the contribution to change you make can relate to attitude or actions. The primary change entails focusing on your child as a unique human being by listening to their perspectives and learning about their interests, rather than concentrating attention on their performance or tasks to complete. Thich Nhat Hanh said, *"When you love someone, the best thing you can offer that person is your presence."*

This could be as simple as not checking every test score or grade. It could involve creating time for engagement with the family or for the exploration of interests out in the community. It could involve a shared meal, a game night, a family meeting about priorities, activities with neighbors, or whatever. There is no blueprint; the choices you make will be unique to your family's values. We need only keep the intention focused on a culture of respect and love.

For some children, their homes are not safe places—emotionally or physically—and this is why we must create human-scale social infrastructure in our local neighborhoods and communities to provide support. As discussed in this book, keeping children confined to systems does not necessarily provide physical or mental safety, and in many ways, it can limit their ability to build supportive networks and explore meaningful possibilities. It is through open ecosystems of interconnected relationships that our children learn and grow.

Regardless of whether you want to start in your home or with other members of your community, it is important to ensure that you have support from one or two other non-spousal people. You need as much support as your children do—your health and well-being have a direct impact on the health and well-being of your children. That support will come from authentic connections. We are not made to go it alone.

B-Unbound Clubs or Centers (for youth)

As discussed in Chapter 6, B-Unbound Clubs are advisory groups that support youth in navigating their way. Parents, educators, and community members can train as Co-Navigators. You can collectively decide to become formally affiliated with the B-Unbound platform or do it on your own (using a different name, as B-Unbound is trademarked). The purpose of the club or center is to provide community youth with peers and adult support—regardless of where (or whether) they attend school.

Although they want to be seen as a unique individual, few teens or young adults want to be that different from their friends. These clubs or centers can provide a home base for them to be with peers as they learn to navigate their own way together. They can learn from each other's experiences as they venture out into the community and connect with supportive adults who share their interests. These clubs or centers can be especially beneficial for youth whose home lives are insecure or whose community environments are unsafe.

Some suggested steps to start:

1. Find a group of youths and parents who are interested in starting a club or center.

2. Identify which parents are interested in training as Co-Navigators.

3. Find a meeting place that is accessible, such as a library, museum, shopping center, park, community center, coffee shop, or any other local community space.

4. Determine the frequency and timing of the gatherings.

5. Set up protocols for monitoring the connections of minors.

6. Determine the agenda. Include story-sharing from guests who have navigated their own way to finding meaningful hobbies or work. This could include Big Picture Learning students or alumni or other interest-based speakers. Although adult mentors can speak sometimes, it is always inspiring for young people to hear from other young people.

7. As they begin to explore possibilities, Navigators can share their explorations with each other.

8. The clubs can also engage in bonding activities such as building things together, making videos, and so on.

9. Once the club gets going, mini-exhibitions with invited family, friends, and mentors can showcase the navigation process and lessons learned.

10. If interested, club members could utilize the IBPLC (BPL's authentic assessment tool described in Chapter 5) to develop a digital portfolio of their experiences.

B-Unbound Circles (for parents)

These self-organized groups can be created with parents in your neighborhood or those you meet through school, extracurricular activities, or work. The people joining the group should have a common interest in supporting each other as their children learn to be the drivers of their own learning with parents occupying the passenger seat. This mission-focused circle is similar to other groups that self-organize to provide support to each other around a common issue, such as Alcoholics Anonymous and others.

Friendships are often found when we realize that we are not the only ones with a particular condition, experience, or viewpoint. "You too!" is a powerful connector. Releasing our children into the world, first with support, then on their own, is scary. We need to support each other in shifting the paradigm. Gathering information is good, but connecting for action is better. Here are some steps to get started:

1. Identify other interested parents by inviting a few people and asking them to invite others. Ideally, the circles are composed of no more than ten to twelve parents. Larger groups can meet together and then break into smaller circles.

2. Find a meeting place that is accessible. If it is just a few parents, meeting in homes may work best. Larger groups can meet in libraries, museums, shopping centers, parks, community centers, coffee shops, or any other local community space.

3. Designate a facilitator or co-facilitators to organize and lead the meetings.

4. Create a meeting format that provides structure to the gathering and sets ground rules for respectful engagement.

5. Meet regularly, weekly, bi-weekly, or monthly.

6. Tailor the agenda to the interests of the group. You can discuss this book or other books such as Elliot Washor's *Learning to Leave* or Dennis Littky's *The Big Picture*, watch TED Talks like Sir Ken's, use The Big Idea's Conversation Guide,[4] or invite speakers. Make sure to leave time for sharing and discussion at the end.

7. Keep the focus on what is in your control—yourselves—not on how you will "help" your children. Role modeling is the most effective way to pass along values.

8. Acknowledge the realities of the system and its impact, but try to encourage the group to focus on how you each can responsibly contribute to change. Some people might volunteer to help with childcare, others could run for the school board, and still others could focus on their own homes. All types of contributions are needed.

9. Encourage each other to become Supportive Adults to youth in your community by sharing your interests or hobbies as a mentor, coach, informational interview, or whatever.

10. Help build a database of supportive adults through your personal and professional connections.

B-Unbound Circles or other similar groups can become the supportive oxygen needed for many parents. I hope that you will become inspired to form or join one. This could create powerful change in your community.

Friendship Benches

Friendship Benches (described in Chapter 7) offer the opportunity for human-to-human connection within local communities. They can be vital lifelines of support. Friendship Benches are typically located in easily accessible areas like parks or community gardens and are staffed by people who live in the community. They have been shown to be more beneficial than institutional support for those suffering from loneliness and depression. For more acute situations, a healthcare clinic or hospital may be needed. These Benches, offering local community engagement and connection, can help reduce the need for institutional care and relieve our overburdened healthcare system. Human-to-human connection is a powerful antidote for distress.

The Friendship Bench model can be applied to more than just mental healthcare. For example, grandmothers (or other community members) could sit on Benches, watching children as a form of childcare. They would not organize or lead activities but would be there for emotional support and to stop the bleeding if anything happened. The children could play freely on their own. The importance of this caregiving role, in community with other grandmothers, could become a very meaningful part of life for all concerned.

AC Groups

For those looking for a more structured therapeutic approach, AC Groups (described in Chapter 7) offer a way for parents, educators, medical professionals, workers, and others to find and give support to one another with guidance from a trained clinician. They are composed of five to six individuals from similar life situations or organizational roles. These groups can provide a buffer during times of adversity and stress. They have been shown to be especially effective for those experiencing burnout by providing them with the tools to build dependable support systems that last over time.

Contribution Apps

The sharing economy (with app-based services such as Airbnb, Uber, and others) has offered new ways for people to generate income from assets they already own. What if we created a contribution economy that allowed for the non-monetary sharing of time and even goods? We have been informally doing this throughout human existence. Victory gardens provided food for many people during World War II. Mutual aid societies, co-ops, and collaboratives have played a vital role at important points in history. Technology has now been developed that can accelerate our ability to create specialized connections, and these apps could support organizing a childcare co-op or even the sharing of food grown in home gardens.

THE POWER OF INTERCONNECTEDNESS

No matter what happens in individual families, our communities have a tremendous impact on whether a child is nurtured or neglected. Too many families, often with only one parent, are isolated and in survival mode. We can create the environments and conditions in our neighborhoods and communities that support all children and their families. The majority of foster youth are removed from their families because of neglect—not enough food, not bathed, and so on. What would happen if neighbors contributed to ensuring that those youth had the care they required before they had to be taken away? How do we connect so we even know that help is needed?

We all have a strong desire for interconnectedness. It is essential for our survival. Our silos and separation have impeded this basic human need. Isolation, whether permanent or temporary, has an impact on well-being, regardless of age or socio-economic status. I saw it at the foster care sibling camp where I volunteered and with the moms in my community facing a new chapter when their children were going off to college.

I have seen firsthand how social connectedness can promote hope and joy. In 2019, a friend asked me if I would host a party to sell Purpose Jewelry made by women survivors of human trafficking. I felt awkward asking women, who often give so much of themselves to their families, schools, workplaces, and communities, to come to my home to buy something without having them receive something in return. I thought that the most valuable thing I could give them was social interaction around a common cause. I suggested a new approach that would offer a variety of ways for these women to gain exposure to human trafficking and, if desired, get involved.

Although I am not a crafty person, I always liked the concept of the old-fashioned quilting bee, where women would gather together and share thoughts, challenges, and insights while they worked on a quilt. I suggested creating a program called Hands of Freedom, where we could support the survivors by packaging the jewelry for the non-profit; our hands would be connected to theirs through the jewelry we all touched. No one would have to buy anything; showing up was enough. Beyond that, they could contribute however they wished.

I invited 100 women to my home on a Wednesday night in the middle of the summer, and 60 showed up. They learned about the prevalence of human trafficking, even in our own community. They also had the opportunity to support survivors by buying jewelry, volunteering as a tutor, sharing on social media, or just talking about it to others. The evening was a huge success, and many new friends were made. The program grew rapidly to hundreds of participants as other women hosted at their homes, churches, workplaces, or community centers.

The concept of gathering together around a common cause can be a way to pioneer a new tomorrow for all children. When our land-line phone systems became limited by global expansion, we did not double down on improving landlines—we built an entirely new cellular system. We need to build the equivalent of the cellular network to support each other and create new opportunities for education, only this network will involve humans living and working in the community.

We already have the physical space needed for this in the form of libraries, community centers, businesses, parks, and, most of all, empty shopping mall spaces and storefronts. These spaces where communities interact can play a vital role in the health and well-being of the individuals within the community. We don't have to build new spaces to create the social infrastructure that nurtures human potential; we need only repurpose existing spaces.

In his book, *Palaces for the People: How Social Infrastructure Can Help Fight Inequality, Polarization, and the Decline of Civic Life*, sociologist Eric Klinenberg, describes the devastating heat wave in Chicago in which many people died.[5] At first glance, it looked like affluent areas fared better than poor areas. But, when he began to investigate further, he saw that those in poor areas where people knew, checked on, and supported each other had higher survival rates than some more affluent areas. The way we live and interact affects our sense of belonging, safety, and health. Providing community support is everyone's business.

Human-scale environments where people know each other promote safety, trust, and responsibility. The magnitude of our societal challenges compared to the smallness of our individual humanness can feel overwhelming. But each of us, joining together to create the collective, can help determine the direction of our society. When we constrain possibilities for meaningful exploration and discovery, we constrain potential contributions and increase cultural disease. Loneliness and meaninglessness are not medical or psychological problems—although they can manifest into them—they are social problems. It is within our control to do something about these.

We cannot wait for someone else to begin and not everyone can or will participate—but each of us who feels compelled to do something can start. The palatable stress of life that existed before the COVID-19 pandemic has only increased. The nuclear family operating in isolation is not how humans are designed to live. By strengthening our community relationships and shifting our cultural narrative around preparing children for a meaningful life, we can create environments that help relieve the overwhelming burden placed on individual families and the systems upon which we have come to depend.

If we are living our lives engaged in meaningful endeavors in collaboration with others, would we be glued to electronic devices? Would we want to watch a simulation of life on TV, or would we want to be living it? We don't need to ban everything we see that scares us. We can make their appeal irrelevant in our lives because we value authentic connection more. We can teach our children how to discern good content from bad rather than policing their screen time. We can show them that real-life engagement is much more desirable. We can build communities where they can belong.

Large, centralized industries, from healthcare to entertainment, have unbundled their services to reach people more effectively. (Because of their captive audience and steady government funding, schools are the singular exception.) Rather than having to go to the doctor's office for all our needs, we can go to a clinic or even a pharmacy for many healthcare needs. Rather than having to buy an entire record, we can now choose individual songs and make our own playlists. Rather than having to go to a theater to see films only when they are released, we can now enjoy them in the comfort of our homes on a variety of streaming platforms. It is possible to take this approach with schooling as well.

Book-smart is not the same as life-smart, and knowledge without experience is just content. Yes, we can learn from the past, but if we use historical data to analyze the future, we are just iterating off the past and creating new versions of the same paradigm. We need to look at new possibilities. We need to adopt life-smart values, not book-smart values. **We don't have to know everything; we just need to know each other.**

Experience shows that knowledge of the past does not forecast the future. Instead, our choices do. Our children need to be ready for life with all its opportunities and challenges. An all-school-no-experience approach has not produced healthy, wealthy, and wise young people. They must concurrently have one foot in the real world and one foot in a learning environment to truly see how the world works and find a meaningful way to contribute to it. In the end, isn't that the goal of education?

Transitions are often difficult to see until we are past them, but we are definitely well into a new era. The emergence of twenty-first-century person-to-person networks has given us new freedom in the ways we can engage and interact. Everything and everyone are inter-dependent and interconnected. Our existence, interwoven with every living thing on our planet, makes us responsible for contributing to the greater good for the health and well-being of all. We are each other's keepers.

We determine what tomorrow looks like. To move from old cultural narratives to new ones, we must envision a new story. What do we want our new story to be? Do we want it to relate to individual status, wealth, and perpetual economic growth based on consumption? Or do we want it to relate to the dignity and value of each individual and our interconnectedness and responsibility to each other and our planet? **We may not be free from the societal conditions we find ourselves in, but we are free to choose how we respond to them.** Our attitudes, decisions, and actions about how we choose to live can create energetic ripples that spread out in all directions.

Human life is messy. It is fraught with suffering, guilt, death, inequity, and fear. But it also has meaning, joy, beauty, possibilities, and, most importantly, love. Love is the most powerful force in the world. It is in transforming our love into action for the sake of issues we care about and people who matter to us that we contribute to life. We have the power to choose to live a different way.

The first post I offered on my blog was not written by me. It was a poem by Kahlil Gibran called "On Children" from his book, *The Prophet*:

Your children are not your children.
They are the sons and daughters of Life's longing for itself.
They come through you but not from you,
And though they are with you yet they belong not to you.

You may give them your love but not your thoughts,
For they have their own thoughts.

You may house their bodies but not their souls,
For their souls dwell in the house of tomorrow, which you cannot visit,
not even in your dreams.

You may strive to be like them, but seek not to make them like you.
For life goes not backward nor tarries with yesterday.
You are the bows from which your children as living arrows
are sent forth.

The archer sees the mark upon the path of the infinite, and He bends
you with His might that His arrows may go swift and far.
Let your bending in the archer's hand be for gladness;
For even as He loves the arrow that flies, so He loves also the bow that
is stable.

We are the bows that send our children forth into the world as their own deciding beings. They do not belong to us; they belong to the future they will help create. As we transcend ourselves by contributing to the change we hope to see, our children will be free to explore the possibilities available to them. They can be the drivers with us in the passenger seat. Our respect, trust, and love for them will be conveyed through the cultural environments we create to nurture and sustain them.

Life can only be seen looking back. The future is uncertain, unknown, and unknowable. "*There is nothing permanent except change,*" said Heraclitus. We are the ones collectively shaping the next moment. We must live our lives like we are shooting frames of a movie—a movie that can only be viewed at the end of our lives. Will we be proud of how we have chosen to live?

My daughters have all navigated their way to the early chapters of their adulthoods. Each of them found their initial job through their own efforts, not through the institutions they attended. They sent countless résumés that ultimately led nowhere, but they persevered by letting everyone they knew know about their interests. Emily is in a high-demand field (pediatric speech therapy) and found her placement through a speech therapist friend who told her about the job opening. Rachel works for a large toy company, where she previously interned. She found the internship through a friend who worked there. She uses her free time to pursue her passion for writing screenplays and TV series. Allison is working at her dream job for a large fashion house in New York City. She found it through a childhood friend's older sister, who knew someone who used to work there. My daughters continue to muddle through good and bad days like all of us, but they have each found meaningful endeavors and supportive communities in their present situations. I am proud and honored to sit in their passenger seats.

Now that my children are grown and out on their own, I am devoting more of my time and energy to my collaborations. I do not know the outcome of any of my endeavors; I just intuitively know they are what I am meant to contribute. When we try to control outcomes in our uncertain world, we can suffer disappointment and miss seeing potential opportunities that may have come into our lives. I used to live my life fixated on specific future goals. Now, I trust my conscience to guide me and respond to the intuitive pull I feel toward people, ideas, and places with my mission as my directional compass. My work has given me meaning and purpose and enriched my life immeasurably.

I hope this book inspires you to contribute your unique self to the mission at hand. Together, we can *make this world worthy of its children*," as Spanish cellist Pablo Casals implored humanity.[6] In small and large ways, we can contribute to turning our cultural tide toward human and planetary flourishing—this can happen in our homes, schools, and communities. The highest human achievement is the ability to transcend ourselves for a greater purpose. This requires us to decide to participate. Are you ready?

Buckle up and enjoy the ride!

———

ACKNOWLEDGMENTS

This book would not have come to be without the encouragement and support of Elliot Washor. He read each chapter as I wrote, offered invaluable insights, and commented on the never-ending title suggestions and cover ideas I sent his way. I am thankful for his friendship and mentorship. I am also grateful to Carlos Moreno, Andrew Frishman, Dennis Littky, and the rest of the Big Picture Learning family for welcoming me into their fold.

As I began writing the book, an introduction to Jules Manuel Villanueva-Castaño led to an unexpected friendship and thought partner. I mentioned the book during a meeting, and he immediately offered to review it. Chapter by chapter, he shared comments and perspectives based on his extensive experience with youth mental health and well-being. Jules worked for years as a behavioral health specialist, youth advocate, and peer group facilitator, and he has interacted with parents and teens in crisis across the socio-economic spectrum. In addition to being the father of two teenagers, his Native American and Chicano heritage afforded me a fresh viewpoint. His contributions enhanced this book, and I appreciate all the time and attention he gave to it.

My sister Cynthia Manfre walked with me every step of the way. She reviewed the book drafts as they were edited. I sent her title ideas and book cover concepts morning and night, and she thoughtfully considered each one and gave her opinion. I am blessed to be related to her.

The steadfast support of many dear friends kept me motivated throughout the writing of this book and I am indebted to them. I am especially appreciative of Kellie Redden, whose enthusiastic support for my writing was affirming and who reviewed multiple word edits, covers, and title ideas. Moira Hummel, who has been in my passenger seat for decades, viewed and commented on multiple drafts, and her husband, Brian, is continually supportive of my work. Margarita Solazzo has played a significant role in my collaborations, and I treasure her friendship. She read early drafts and sent innumerable title ideas. They have all been champions of my mission for many years and I am grateful to know them.

I am thankful for the support, friendship, and mentorship of Alex Vesely-Frankl. I relied on him to ensure that I stayed true to his grandfather's philosophies. We discussed language and wording in detail. He also provided feedback on the innumerable titles I suggested and provided some of his own.

Many early manuscript readers provided invaluable feedback: Ann Geary, Heather David, Amanda Jacobson, Eileen Medrano, Marisa Polvino, Trevor Davis, Trinity Wallace-Ellis, Peter Hostrawser, Tim Salau, Tracie Spence, and Maddie Gillissie. I am appreciative of the final draft and cover feedback I received from Monica Snellings, Kim Turner, Wendy Dailey, Cathleen Larson, Karen Jordan, Carrie McLain, and Bryan Jacobson. I am grateful to Cara Cragun, who not only reviewed the book but again contributed her talent to developing the logo, website, and social media presence.

I am "co" everything. My life has been enriched by the many partnerships I have formed and the friendships that have emerged. I would like to acknowledge my fellow collaborators: Kate Cohen, Marisa Polvino, and Katie Menke of Straight Up Impact; Elliot Washor and Anthonette Peña of B-Unbound; the late Suniya Luthar and Kimber Bogard of AC Groups; Dixon Chibanda, Bill Roy, and Graham Leader of The Friendship Bench film; and Ahmed Labbate and Amar Santana of Vaca Restaurant.

I relied on the editing and publishing team of Nikki Van De Car, Nirmala Nataraj, Jennifer Sanders, Audra Figgins, Elisabeth Rinaldi, and Christina Thiele at KN Literary Arts to help prepare this book for readers. Their professional care and attention in ensuring my messages were communicated in an understandable manner and readable form are greatly appreciated.

Johann Hari inspired me to share my voice and challenge social narratives. His courage to present alternative perspectives opened the door for me and many others to do the same. I value his friendship and support.

My mother, sister Robin, and brother-in-law Bryan have always aided my endeavors and encouraged me to speak my truth. My nephews, nieces, and all the extra kids I have "adopted" over the years have also blessed my life.

I am grateful to my former husband, Paul Roy, whose unwavering support and trust in my many choices and decisions for our daughters led to the experiences and lessons I share in this book. His love for our family is ever-present. We are both incredibly proud of the young women our daughters have become and share a continued commitment to their well-being. We are excited that our family is expanding with the addition of Emily's soon-to-be husband, Jacob Terpstra, who has enriched all our lives.

My love for my daughters, Emily, Rachel, and Allison, cannot be reduced to mere words. They have given my life meaning and purpose beyond anything I could have imagined. The highs and lows we've shared have created an unbreakable bond. I value the uniqueness of each of them and am eternally grateful for the joy they bring to my life.

I have had the pleasure of interacting with many parents and kids over the years who provided fuel to my mission. The pain in our society is palatable. I appreciate the trust and courage of the kids who have reached out to me for guidance and mentorship and the parents who have shared their stories with me. I wrote this book for all of them.

NOTES

INTRODUCTION

1   U.S. Bureau of Labor Statistics, "Occupational Employment and Wages—
     May 2016," U.S. Department of Labor, March 31, 2017, bls.gov/news.
     release/archives/ocwage_03312017.pdf.

2   Digest of Education Statistics, "Median annual earnings of full-time
     year-round workers 25 to 34 years old and full-time year-round workers
     as a percentage of the labor force, by sex, race/ethnicity, and educational
     attainment: Selected years, 1995 through 2016," National Center for
     Education Statistics, October 2017, nces.ed.gov/programs/digest/d17/
     tables/dt17_502.30.asp.

3   American School Counselor Association, "Student-to-School-Counselor-
     Ratio" Ratio 2020–2021," U.S. Department of Education, 2021,
     schoolcounselor.org/getmedia/238f136e-ec52-4bf2-94b6-f24c39447022/
     Ratios-20-21-Alpha.pdf.

CHAPTER 1

1   Ross Brenneman, "Gallup Student Poll Finds Engagement in School
     Dropping by Grade Level," Education Week, March 22, 2016, edweek.
     org/leadership/gallup-student-poll-finds-engagement-in-school-dropping-
     by-grade-level/2016/03.

2   Jon Clifton, "The Real Global Job Crisis," Gallup, accessed June 13, 2023,
     gallup.com/analytics/471212/real-global-jobs-crisis.aspx.

3   Lou Adler, "New Survey Reveals 85% of All Jobs are Filled Via
     Networking," LinkedIn, February 28, 2016, linkedin.com/pulse/
     new-survey-reveals-85-all-jobs-filled-via-networking-lou-adler.

4   Gina Belli, "How Many Jobs Are Found Through Networking,
     Really?" Payscale, April 6, 2017, payscale.com/career-advice/
     many-jobs-found-networking.

5   U.S. Bureau of Labor Statistics, "Employee Tenure Summary," U.S.
     Department of Labor, September 22, 2022, bls.gov/news.release/tenure.
     nr0.htm.

6   "The Gig Economy Goes Global," Morgan Stanley, May 8, 2018, morgan-stanley.com/ideas/freelance-economy.

7   Eric Barker, "Wondering What Happened to Your Class Valedictorian? Not Much, Research Shows," Money, May 18, 2017, money.com/valedictorian-success-research-barking-up-wrong.

8   Todd Rose, toddrose.com.

9   "Autism in the Workforce: Companies Hiring People with Autism," International Board of Credentialing and Continuing Education Standards, September 10, 2019, ibcces.org/blog/2019/09/10/autism-workforce-hiring; Kate Griggs, "Dyslexic Thinking Is Now Officially Recognized as a Valuable Skill!" March 31, 2022, linkedin.com/pulse/dyslexic-thinking-now-officially-recognised-valuable-skill-griggs.

10 AMA Staff, "New Research Reveals Many Entrepreneurs Are Dyslexic," American Management Association, January 24, 2019, amanet.org/articles/new-research-reveals-many-entrepreneurs-are-dyslexic.

11 U.S. Bureau of Labor Statistics, "Occupational Employment and Wages News Release," U.S. Department of Labor, March 31, 2021, bls.gov/news.release/archives/ocwage_03312021.htm.

12 Oren Cass, "How the Other Half Learns: Reorienting an Education System That Fails Most Students," Manhattan Institute, August 28, 2018, manhattan-institute.org/html/how-other-half-learns-reorienting-education-system-fails-most-students-11419.html.

13 "The Labor Market for Recent Graduates," Federal Reserve Bank of New York, May 4, 2023, newyorkfed.org/research/college-labor-market/index.html#underemployment. Over the past decade, about 40% were typically underemployed.

14 Mark Kantrowitz, "Shocking Statistics About College Graduation Rates," Forbes, November 18, 2021, forbes.com/sites/markkantrowitz/2021/11/18/shocking-statistics-about-college-graduation-rates/?sh=4e0caffa2b69; Doug Shapiro, Afet Dundar, Phoebe Khasiala Wakhungu, Xin Yuan, Angel Nathan, and Youngsik Hwang, "Time to Degree: A National View of the Time Enrolled and Elapsed for Associate and Bachelor's Degree Earners (Signature Report No. 11),"

National Student Clearinghouse Research Center, September 2016, nscre-searchcenter.org/wp-content/uploads/SignatureReport11.pdf.

15   Winnie Hu, Kellen Browning, and Karen Zraick, "Uber Partners with Yellow Taxi Companies in N.Y.C.," *The New York Times*, March 29, 2022, nytimes.com/2022/03/24/business/uber-new-york-taxis.html.

16   Nick Skillicorn, "Evidence That Children Become Less Creative Over Time (And How to Fix It)," Idea to Value, August 5, 2016, ideatovalue.com/crea/nickskillicorn/2016/08/ evidence-children-become-less-creative-time-fix.

17   Liz Mineo, "Good Genes Are Nice, but Joy Is Better," *The Harvard Gazette*, April 11, 2017, news.harvard.edu/gazette/story/2017/04/ over-nearly-80-years-harvard-study-has-been-showing-how-to-live-a-healthy-and-happy-life.

CHAPTER 2

1   Benjamin Hansen, Joseph J. Sabia, and Jessamyn Schaller, "In-Person Schooling and Youth Suicide: Evidence from School Calendars and Pandemic School Closures," National Bureau of Economic Research, December 2022, nber.org/papers/w30795.

2   "Suicide in Children and Teens," American Academy of Child and Adolescent Psychiatry, June 2012, aacap.org/AACAP/Families_and_ Youth/Facts_for_Families/FFF-Guide/Teen-Suicide-010.aspx.

3   "Facts About Suicide," Centers for Disease Control and Prevention, May 8, 2023, cdc.gov/suicide/facts/index.html.

4   Brianna Hansen, "The Pursuit of Positivity in the Workplace: Q&A with Happiness Expert Shawn Achor," Wrike, May 9, 2021, wrike.com/blog/ workplace-positivity-shawn-achor-interview.

5   "The Life of Viktor Frankl," The Viktor E. Frankl Institute of America, accessed June 13, 2023, viktorfranklamerica.com/viktor-frankl-bio.

6   Viktor Frankl, *The Feeling of Meaninglessness: A Challenge to Psychotherapy and Philosophy* (Milwaukee, Wisconsin: Marquette University Press, 2010), 182.

7   Find information about B-Unbound at b-unbound.org.

8   "Declaration of the Rights of the Child," United Nations General Assembly, Fourteenth Session, 1959, digitallibrary.un.org/record/195831.

9   Frankl, *The Feeling of Meaninglessness*, 183.

10   Frankl, *The Feeling of Meaninglessness*, 203.

11   Frankl, *The Feeling of Meaninglessness*, 141.

12   Rebecca Rashid and Arthur C. Brooks, "How to Know You're Lonely," *The Atlantic*, October 12, 2021, theatlantic.com/podcasts/archive/2021/10/howto-friendship-loneliness-arthurbrooks-vivekmurthy-happiness/620281.

13   "Loneliness," *Psychology Today*, accessed June 13, 2023, psychologytoday.com/us/basics/loneliness.

14   Karen Guzman, "U.S. Surgeon General Vivek H. Murthy '03 Discusses the Loneliness Epidemic," Yale School of Management, September 13, 2022, som.yale.edu/story/2022/us-surgeon-general-vivek-h-murthy-03-discusses-loneliness-epidemic.

15   "Chronic Diseases in America," Centers for Disease Control and Prevention, December 13, 2022, cdc.gov/chronicdisease/resources/infographic/chronic-diseases.htm.

16   Sari Harrar, "Inside America's Psychiatrist Shortage," Psycom, October 1, 2019, psycom.net/inside-americas-psychiatrist-shortage.

CHAPTER 3

1   After his death, Patrick's family created the Patrick's Purpose Foundation to support mental health and wellness in schools. Find out more at patrickspurposefoundation.org.

2   Nassim Nicholas Taleb, *Antifragile: Things That Gain from Disorder* (New York: Random House, 2012).

3   Find out more about Jo's work at joboaler.org.

4   John Dewey, *The School and Society* (New York: Cosimo Classics, 2008).

5   Gavin de Becker, *Protecting the Gift: Keeping Children and Teenagers Safe (and Parents Sane)* (New York: The Dial Press, 1999).

6   Lenore Skenazy, "Let's Pass Some More Free-Range Parenting Laws in 2021!" Free-Range Kids, December 31, 2020, freerangekids.com/lets-pass-some-more-free-range-parenting-laws-in-2021.

CHAPTER 4

1   David Hildebrand, "John Dewey," *The Stanford Encyclopedia of Philosophy*, edited by Edward N. Zalta and Uri Nodelman, forthcoming fall 2023.

2   Find out more about Trinity's work at trinityspeaks.com.

3   Clayton M. Christensen, James Allworth, and Karen Dillon, *How Will You Measure Your Life?* (New York: HarperCollins, 2012).

4   Find out more at petergray.org.

5   Peter Gray, "The Culture of Childhood: We've Almost Destroyed It," Psychology Today, October, 31, 2016, psychologytoday.com/us/blog/freedom-learn/201610/the-culture-childhood-we-ve-almost-destroyed-it.

6   Taleb, *Antifragile*, 204.

7   Find out more about Authentic Connections Group at acgroups.org.

8   Ken Robinson, "Sir Ken Robinson with Herb Kim, Interview Part Two," August 27, 2014, TEDx Talks, youtube.com/watch?v=wKTMSMr3Q5k&ab_channel=TEDxTalks.

9   Roman Krznaric, *How to Find Fulfilling Work* (New York: Picador, 2013).

CHAPTER 5

1   Find out more about Education Reimagined at education-reimagined.org.

2   Find out more about Big Picture Learning at bigpicture.org.

3   Elliot Washor, Andrew Frishman, and Eva Mcjia, "Findings from the Big Picture Learning Longitudinal Study," Education Reimagined, January 26, 2021, education-reimagined.org/findings-from-the-big-picture-learning-longitudinal-study.

4   Karen Arnold and Georgiana Mihut, "Post-Secondary Outcomes of
     Innovative High Schools: The Big Picture Longitudinal Study," Teachers
     College Record Vol. 122, No. 8, October 21, 2020, esri.ie/publications/
     post-secondary-outcomes-of-innovative-high-schools-the-big-picture-lon-
     gitudinal-study.

CHAPTER 6

1   David J. Deming and Kadeem L. Noray, "STEM Careers and the
     Changing Requirements of Work," National Bureau of Economic
     Research, June 2019, nber.org/papers/w25065.

2   Find out more about the Christensen Institute's work at
     christenseninstitute.org/blog/topics/social-capital.

3   Julia Freeland Fisher, "Students' Hidden Networks: Relationship Mapping
     as a Strategy to Build Asset-Based Pathways," The Clayton Christensen
     Institute for Disruptive Innovation, August 2022, christenseninstitute.org/
     wp-content/uploads/2022/08/Relationship_Mapping.pdf.

4   Peter Gray, "Why Kids Ares Suffering Today," Psychology Today,
     March 30, 2022, psychologytoday.com/us/blog/freedom-learn/202203/
     why-kids-are-suffering-today.

5   Find out more about Bluedoor Community at bluedoor.community.

6   Find out more about Habitat for Aviation at habitatforaviation.org.

7   This sentiment is attributed to Mead in Paul Brand and Philip Yancey,
     *Fearfully and Wonderfully Made: A Surgeon Looks at the Human and
     Spiritual Body* (Grand Rapids, Michigan: Zondervan Publishing House,
     1980).

CHAPTER 7

1   Find out more about the Friendship Bench at friendshipbenchzimbabwe.
     org.

2   Dixon Chibanda et. al., "Effect of a Primary Care–Based Psychological
     Intervention on Symptoms of Common Mental Disorders in Zimbabwe:
     A Randomized Clinical Trial," *The Journal of the American Medical*

Association Vol. 316, No. 24, December 27, 2016, jamanetwork.com/journals/jama/fullarticle/2594719.

3   Find out more about Beyond the Race to Nowhere at beyondtheracetonowhere.org.

4   Find out more about Johann's work at johannhari.com.

5   Find information about Bruce K. Alexander and the Rat Park experiments at brucekalexander.com/articles-speeches/rat-park.

6   Johann, Hari, Lost Connections: *Uncovering the Real Causes of Depression—and the Unexpected Solutions* (New York: Bloomsbury USA, 2018).

7   Johann Hari, "The Real Causes of Depression Have Been Discovered, and They're Not What You Think," The Huffington Post, January 28, 2018, huffpost.com/entry/opinion-hari-depression-causes_n_5a6a144de4b0ddb658c46a21.

8   Johann Hari, "This Could Be Why You Are Depressed or Anxious," TED, TEDSummit 2019, ted.com/talks/johann_hari_this_could_be_why_you_re_depressed_or_anxious?language=en.

9   Find out more about Classroom Without Walls at classroomwithoutwalls.ai/welcome-page.

10   Find out more about Peter's work at peterhostrawser.com.

11   Peter Hostrawser, "Great Teachers Are Not Superheroes," Peter Hostrawser, December 1, 2022, peterhostrawser.com/blog/great-teachers-are-not-superheroes.

12   Find out more about Ziz's work at 43fortycoaching.com.

13   Find out more about Tim's work at timsalau.com.

14   Find out more about Suniya's work at suniyaluthar.org.

15   S. S. Luthar and L. Ciciolla, L., "Who Mothers Mommy? Factors that Contribute to Mothers' Well-Being," *Developmental Psychology* Vol. 51, No. 12, 1812–23, psycnet.apa.org/doi/10.1037/dev0000051.

16   Find out more about the Big Idea at thebigidea.education-reimagined.org.

17   Kelly Young, "A Note from Education Reimagined," *Voyager*, January 27, 2022, *education-reimagined.org/voyager/january-2022.*

18   Find out more about VELA Education Fund at velaedfund.org.

CHAPTER 8

1   John D. Krumboltz, "The Happenstance Learning Theory," *Journal of Career Assessment* Vol. 17, Issue 2, May 2009, doi. org/10.1177/1069072708328861.

2   Name has been changed to protect privacy.

CHAPTER 9

1   Fred Rogers, *The Mister Rogers' Parenting Book: Helping to Understand Your Young Child* (Philadelphia, Pennsylvania: Running Press, 2002).

2   Marianna McMurdock, "Black Mothers Launch Microschools to End School-Prison Pipeline," Yahoo! News, January 26, 2022, yahoo.com/ video/black-mothers-launch-microschools-end-121500237.html.

3   Jeremiah Poff, "'School Choice Revolution': Utah Becomes Third State to Enact Universal Program," *Washington Examiner*, January 30, 2023, washingtonexaminer.com/restoring-america/community-family/school-choice-revolution-utah-becomes-third-state-to-enact-universal-program.

4   "Explore What's Possible: A Conversation Guide to a Community-Based Ecosystem of Learning Approach," Education Reimagined, April 2022, thebigidea.education-reimagined.org/wp-content/uploads/2022/04/ERI-Conversation-Guide.pdf.

5   Eric Klinenberg, *Palaces for the People: How Social Infrastructure Can Help Fight Inequality, Polarization, and the Decline of Civic Life* (New York: Crown Publishing, 2019).

6   Maria Popova, " Make This World Worthy of Its Children: Legendary Cellist Pau Casals on JFK, Violence, the Proper Aim of Education, and the Measure of Our Humanity," *The Marginalian*, March 10, 2016, quoting from *Pablo Casals, Joys and Sorrows* (New York: Simon and Schuster, 1970).

INDEX

ABOUT THE AUTHOR

Pam Roy is a writer, filmmaker, investor, and philanthropist with a mission to provide community-based support for youth and families. Her passion for parenting and educational transformation is inspired by her three daughters, now young adults. What started as a parenting blog (pamroyblog.com) evolved into co-founding several organizations and initiatives. She is the co-founder of Straight Up Impact (a women-owned production company at the intersection of film and social impact) and B-Unbound (an initiative with Big Picture Learning that connects youth with community-based adults who share their interests).

Recognizing the key role meaning plays in mental health, Pam also co-founded the Viktor E. Frankl Institute of America with Frankl's grandson, Alexander Vesely-Frankl. It provides resources related to meaning-oriented theory and philosophy. She co-authored *The Inspiring Wisdom of Viktor Frankl: A 21-Day Reflection Book About Meaning* with Moira Hummel and developed a course with Alexander called *Viktor Frankl's Logotherapy: The Discovery of Meaning* (offered on the website and Udemy). She is an executive producer of the forthcoming feature film adapted from Frankl's internationally best-selling book *Man's Search for Meaning*.

In addition, Pam is an executive producer of The Friendship Bench documentary based on Dixon Chibanda's TED Talk about training grandmothers to treat depression. She is an advisor to Dixon and is working with him to put Friendship Benches on every corner. Pam is on the board of AC Groups, which promotes people's resilience and reduces workplace burnout. Lastly, she is co-owner of Vaca Restaurant Group with Ahmed Labbate and Chef Amar Santana.

MORE INFORMATION

Passenger Seat Parent

To connect with Pam and learn more about resources related to the book, please go to *PassengerSeatParent.com*

Find out about the initiatives and organizations discussed in the book at the following websites:

B-Unbound.org
ViktorFranklAmerica.com
StraightUpImpact.com
FriendshipBenchZimbabwe.org
ACGroups.org
PamRoyBlog.com

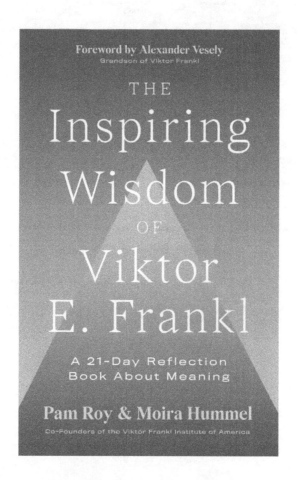

The Inspiring Wisdom of Viktor E. Frankl:
A 21-Day Reflection Book About Meaning
(Written with Moira Hummel)

Printed in the USA
CPSIA information can be obtained
at www.ICGtesting.com
JSHW021935260124
56108JS00002BB/2